Corporation
Get You

*Globalization and the Downsizing
of the American Dream*

Edited by Kevin Danaher

Common Courage Press
Monroe, Maine

Common Courage Press
Box 702
Monroe, Maine 04951
Phone: (207) 525-0900
FAX: (207) 525-3068

Cover by Matt Wuerker
Book design by Kevin Danaher

Library of Congress Cataloging-In-Publication Data

Corporations are gonna get your mama: globalization and the
downsizing of the American dream / edited by Kevin Danaher.
         p.   cm.
   ISBN 1-56751-113-9 (cloth). -- ISBN 1-56751-112-0 (paper)
   1. International business enterprises--Moral and ethical aspects.
2. Cost and standard of living--United States. 3. United States--
economic conditions--1981- 4. Environmental protection. 5.
Political participation--United States.   I. Danaher, Kevin.
HD2755.5.C654   1997
338.8'8--dc20   96-31851
                                                              CIP

Contents

Acknowledgments

First and foremost, I want to thank all the members of our growing family here at Global Exchange: what kind of heaven is it to get up in the morning and *want* to go to work!?! My deep gratitude goes out to Rick Rowden, Corey Oser, Josh Shimkin, Jessica Siff, Chloe Osmer and Paige Harrison who helped with scanning, editing, proofreading and general decision-making that was indispensable to the production of this book. Big thanks also to Greg Bates of Common Courage for critical feedback, good ideas and a positive attitude.

Special thanks to our friends at the Foundation for Deep Ecology who provided the funding that made this book possible.

Big hugs and kisses to Medea, Arlen and Maya, whose daily doses of love and affection keep me on track and happy.

Thanks to the following organizations and publications for graciously giving us permission to reprint their work: *The Nation* (Chapters 1, 6 and 12), *New Internationalist* (Chapter 2), *Multinational Monitor* (Chapters 3, 14 and 20), *In These Times* (Chapter 5), Institute for Policy Studies (Chapters 7, 9 and 17), *Monthly Review* (Chapters 8 and 13), *Dollars and Sense* (Chapters 10 and 22), Public Citizen (Chapter 11), *The New York Times* (Chapter 15), People Centered Development Forum (Chapter 18), *Labor Research Review* (Chapter 19), Redefining Progress (Chapter 21).

"Before you finish eating breakfast this morning, you've depended on more than half the world. This is the way our universe is structured... We aren't going to have peace on earth until we recognize this basic fact of the interrelated structure of all reality."

Rev. Martin Luther King, Jr.

Foreword

Debunking the Corporate Agenda

Noam Chomsky

Public attitudes shed interesting light on what is happening in the corridors of power. More than 80 percent of the public feels that the government is "run for the benefit of the few and the special interests, not the people," up from a steady 50 percent for a similarly worded question in earlier years. The same percentages feel that the economic system is "inherently unfair," and that working people have too little say in what is going on in the country. More than 70 percent feel that "Business has gained too much power over too many aspects of American life" and "has benefited more than consumers from government deregulation." Two-thirds say that the "American dream" has become "harder to achieve" since the 1980s. And by what *Business Week* calls "a stunning 95 percent-to-5 percent majority," the public believes that corporations "should sometimes sacrifice some profit for the sake of making things better for their workers and communities."

Such attitudes, novel only in scale, suggest some conclusions about how the population perceives the workings of power. But these are not the conclusions that have regularly been drawn, for example, by the journal that reported in 1992 that 83 percent of the public think that the rich are getting richer, the poor are getting poorer, and the economic system is "inherently unfair." From these facts, we are to conclude that people are angry at "their well-paid politicians" and want "more power to the people," not "more power to the government." That is an intriguing interpretation of the facts reported, though it makes some sense on two essential principles that the doctrinal system has labored to implant in "the public mind": first, government cannot be responsive to public interests; and second, private power does not exist, even though the Fortune 500 control almost two-thirds of the domestic economy and much of the international economy, with an enormous impact throughout the political and ideological institutions, and the society and culture generally.

The official version of reality portrays a conflict between the government, which is necessarily the enemy, and the people, who are living the American dream: the sober working man, his loyal wife (now maybe with a job herself), the hard-working executive toiling for the benefit of all, the friendly banker eager to lend money—all a model of harmony, their happy lives disrupted only by outsiders and un-Americans such as union organizers and other riffraff. That is the tale that has been diligently crafted by the public relations industry from the late 1930s, when the shock of popular organizing shattered the belief that the end of history had been reached in a kind of utopia of the masters. With some variants, the picture has endured in business propaganda, the entertainment industry, and much of the popular and intellectual culture.

It is a tribute to the propaganda system that when the dam finally broke during the 1996 presidential primary campaign, and popular attitudes could no longer be reconstructed to fit the preferred image, there was real surprise and alarm at the appeal on class lines by a demagogue assuming a populist mantle. Republican presidential candidate Pat Buchanan "opened a second front" in the "class war," *New York Times* commentator Jason DeParle reported. Before that, unhappy people were expressing their rage in the approved manner, targeting "welfare families, immigrants, and beneficiaries of affirmative action." But now they were discovering bosses, managers, investors, speculators, even class conflict, much to the amazement of commentators who hadn't noticed these exotic features of our harmonious society.

We may be entering a new "blame era," Meg Greenfield lamented in *Newsweek*, with "a switch from a variety of other organized grievances and conflicts to a developing economic class warfare theme." Many people are seeking "a new national heavy," someone they can blame for their woes. They are confused by the "things happening in that universe that only the specialist can understand" and are coming to focus their "animosity" on "fat cats." That is unfortunate, but understandable, Greenfield explains: misguided people always look for "malign forces...to explain their own failures and miseries," sometimes "Catholics and Jews and immigrants," now "the corporate executives and top-level managers and investment bankers and other movers and shakers and dealmakers in the burgeoning new business universe." "So far, most Americans have tended to blame Big Government for their economic woes," the editors of *Business Week* add, "but now their anger may be shifting in some measure toward Big Business." Many are even challenging "the role of the corporation in society." "Only the foolish would ignore the signs," and corporations must consider "the need to be more responsible corporate citizens" if they are to undercut the "reviving left."

There was still greater shock and distress that the public feels that the masters of the economy are not meeting their responsibility to workers and communities, by a margin of almost twenty to one. The reaction merits some attention.

One should note carefully the range of options admitted into public discussion now that the harmony of the past has been disrupted by the confused and misguided public and cynical politicians. The new broadened spectrum of responsible debate now extends from those who believe that the rulers of the private economy should ruthlessly seek profit, to the other extreme, where it is felt that they should be more benevolent autocrats.

Missing from the spectrum are some other conceivable possibilities: for example, the thoughts of Thomas Jefferson, who warned that the rising "banking institutions and moneyed incorporations" would destroy democracy and restore a form of absolutism if given free rein, as they later were, beyond his worst nightmares. Or of Alexis de Tocqueville, who, like Jefferson and Adam Smith, regarded equality of condition as an important feature of a free and just society, and saw the dangers of a "permanent inequality of conditions" if "the manufacturing aristocracy which is growing up under our eyes" in the United States, and "is one of the harshest that has ever existed in the world," should escape its confines, spelling the end of democracy. Or of America's leading 20th century social philosopher, John Dewey, who held that we cannot talk seriously about democracy in a regime of private power. "Power today resides in control of the means of production, exchange, publicity, transportation and communication," he wrote. "Whoever owns them rules the life of the country," and politics is no more than "the shadow cast on society by big business," as long as the country is ruled by "business for private profit through private control of banking, land, industry, reinforced by command of the press, press agents and other means of publicity and propaganda." To correct this fundamental abuse of freedom and democracy, workers must be "the masters of their own industrial fate," not mere tools rented by employers, a point of view that traces back to the origins of classical liberalism. Until industry is changed "from a feudalistic to a democratic social order," based on workers' control, democratic forms may exist, but their substance will be limited.

Such ideas were also current in the independent working class press from the early days of industrial development in the United States. Working people did not plead with the aristocracy to be more benevolent, but declared it to be illegitimate, denying its right to be harsh or benevolent. They were denying its right to determine what happens in the economic, social, and political world, or on the factory floor. Like Dewey many years later, they insisted that "they who work in the mills ought to own them," so that authentic democracy can be envisaged.

All of this is as American as apple pie, an important part of the authentic history of the United States. But all of this is missing, even as the spectrum broadens to tolerate the idea that the reigning aristocrats should act more kindly to their subjects. At the outer limits some adventurous souls challenge "corporate greed" and contemplate measures to bribe the rulers to be more benevolent, though such extremist ideas are not welcome to corporate America, which "believes in the power of the free market to balance competing interests," we learn in a think-piece on the topic in the *Boston Globe*, or to a "Republican-controlled Congress leery of interfering with free market capitalism"—by such measures as increasing the huge transfer payments from the public to high tech industry through the Pentagon system, for example.

As unthinkable as the idea that pleas to the autocracy to be more benevolent may not reach the outer limits of extremism is the truism that corporate America has always insisted on the traditional version of free market doctrine: for thee, but not for me, except for temporary advantage. I need the protection of the nanny state; you have to learn responsibility under the harsh discipline of the market. U.S. business is, of course, not alone in this regard. To cite just one illustration, a recent study of the top 100 transnationals in the *Fortune* 500 list found that "virtually all appeared to have sought and gained from industrial and/or trade policies [of their home government] at some point," and "at least 20 ... would not have survived as independent companies if they had not been saved in some way by their governments."

There's no need to explain any of this to Gingrich, the Heritage Foundation, Reaganite planners, or other noted "conservatives," who can also rest assured that the scam won't be exposed. Gingrich's success in becoming the country's leading corporate welfare enthusiast goes well beyond dependency on the direct handouts that enrich his constituents. A teacher in Gingrich's federally-funded Cobb County district informs me that the principal of his school instructed teachers each year to pad the federal employee count to maximize the flow of public funds, for example: "If you know that a student's father is a milkman who delivers milk on any federal property (Lockheed, Dobbins Air Force Base, the naval air station, etc.) count him/her as a federal employee." Massachusetts governor William Weld is a libertarian who believes in the free market with religious fervor, the *Boston Globe* assured its readers, reporting a few days later that he had "made a concerted effort to chase every federal dollar in sight," far surpassing his predecessor Michael Dukakis in bringing a huge flow of federal funds to Massachusetts so that he can boast of his fiscal conservatism and ability to keep the state in the black, while making sure that the defenseless undergo the rigors of tough love. The practices are routine.

The standard story, ever since the November 1994 congressional elections, has been that the Newt-Gingrich-free-market enthusiasts were pursuing the poll-driven Contract with America in our pluralistic democracy. From the beginning, it was clear that this was fraud, and the facts are now conceded. The *Chicago Tribune* reported a press conference by Frank Luntz, polling specialist of the Gingrich Republicans, under the headline: "GOP pollster never measured popularity of 'Contract,' only slogans." When Luntz assured reporters that a majority of Americans supported each of the ten parts of the Contract, as they duly reported, what he meant, he now explains, is that a majority liked the slogans that were used for packaging. Thus, studies of focus groups showed that the public opposes dismantling the public health system and wants to "preserve, protect and strengthen" it "for the next generation." So dismantling is packaged as "a solution that preserves and protects Medicare for seniors and that sets the stage for the baby boomers" (Gingrich). Republicans will "preserve and protect" the health system, Bob Dole added.

All of this is very natural in a society that is, to an unusual degree, business-run, with huge expenditures on marketing—$1 trillion a year, one-sixth of 1992 Gross Domestic Product (GDP), according to a recent academic study by Michael Dawson, and almost all tax-deductible, so that the people pay for the privilege of being subjected to manipulation of their attitudes and behavior. These are among the many forms of control and deceit designed to create artificial wants and manipulate "the habits and opinions of the masses," in the words of one of the founders of the Public Relations industry.

None of this is particularly new, except perhaps in scale, and perhaps brazenness, though here some caution is necessary. Deceit has become so entrenched that it may well have been internalized, passing below the threshold of consciousness. Prevailing market rhetoric is an interesting case. Much of the commentary about the dedication of the Reaganites to free markets was tongue-in-cheek, one must assume; it was no secret that they were forging new paths in protectionism and state intervention in the economy. But by now, one begins to wonder.

In *Foreign Affairs*, Joseph Nye, Dean of Harvard's Kennedy School of Government, and Admiral William Owens argue that U.S. global power has been underestimated. Washington's diplomacy has an unnoticed new "ability to achieve desired outcomes in international affairs, a "force multiplier" resulting from "the attraction of American democracy and free markets"; specifically, from "Cold War investments" that enabled U.S. industry to dominate "important communications and information processing technologies." Huge subsidies extracted from the public under the guise of "security"—conscious deception, as we know from the documentary record—are a real tribute to democracy and free markets. Boston international lawyer Larry Schwartz adds further insight: "A pre-eminent group of free-market scholars" has concluded that "Silicon Valley and Route 128" in Boston may illustrate the best way "to implement market principles in former communist economies," thanks to their "interactive system of venture capitalists, entrepreneurs, skilled labor, universities, support services and entrepreneurial and supplier networks"—and public subsidies that are somehow missing from the picture, perhaps because it is simply taken for granted that "free enterprise" means that the task of the public is to pay the costs, and assume the risks if something goes wrong.

Joining those who now perceive the "unprecedented redistribution of income toward the rich," John Cassidy, in a useful report on the tribulations of the "middle class" in the *New Yorker*, concludes that "this is nobody's fault; it is just how capitalism has developed." It is what "the free market has decided, in its infinite but mysterious wisdom," and "politicians will eventually have to wake up and accept the fact," abandoning the pretense that something can be done about forces of nature. His study mentions three corporations: McDonnell Douglas, Grumman, and Hughes Aircraft, all paragons of free market capitalism, no less so than Clinton's choice as he preached his "grand vision" of the free market future (Boeing), or Gingrich's favorite (Lockheed-Martin), or "America's most valuable company" (General Electric), to mention just a few.

This is hardly new. Long ago, England was preaching the wonders of the market to India while despoiling it and massively protecting its own industry and commerce, the course followed by its former American colonies as soon as they were free to pursue an independent path. "Perfection" and "finality" have repeatedly been proclaimed. But with all the sordid continuities, an optimistic soul can—realistically I think—discern slow progress. Popular struggles today can start from a much higher plane and with far greater expectations than those of the Gay '90s and Roaring '20s, or even 30 years ago. There is no more reason now than there has ever been to believe that we are constrained by mysterious and unknown social laws, not simply decisions made within institutions that are subject to human will, as always in the past.

The book you are holding explains why we should be mobilizing against corporate domination. It also documents some of the many ways in which people are organizing resistance and building alternative institutions. Books can be either mere entertainment or useful tools in changing the world. This effort was intended to be the latter, but whether it will play that role or not will be determined by what you do after you put this book down.

Noam Chomsky
July 1996

[Excerpted and adapted from Z magazine, June 1966, and from the transcript of the Cleveland-Marshall Fund Lecture, Cleveland State College of Law, March 1996.]

Introduction: Corporate Power and the Quality of Life

Kevin Danaher

Just about every day we hear something about globalization. The mass media give us the impression that the impersonal forces of the "free market" are knitting together the peoples of the world into a seamless quilt. We are led to believe that things will steadily get better if we can just keep governments from meddling with the market forces that lead to more growth and efficiency.

Yet we know that jobs are being lost to "global competition." We know that the global environment is being threatened on a number of fronts, from global warming and the deterioration of the ozone layer to the extermination of species and the poisoning of the world's water supply. We see refugees and immigrants by the millions roaming the planet, in search of jobs and protection from armed conflict. We also know that inequality is getting worse: Fewer and fewer large corporations own more of the world's productive resources while millions of people are unable to sustain their families. Many of us have a gut feeling that the global economy has gone awry. We would do well to trust our feelings.

But what is the reality behind our feelings of dread? The decline in our standard of living can be seen in numerous areas:

1. As U.S. corporations have expanded their global reach they are better able to put the U.S. workforce in direct competition

with foreign workers, thus increasing their profits while driving down our wages and general standard of living.

2. Global corporations are better able to use technology to downsize their workforces, thus creating anxiety among workers who no longer feel secure about the future of their jobs.

3. As global corporations become less dependent on any particular nation, they have less interest in supporting any government with taxes. This results in a shrinking tax base and what is referred to as a "fiscal crisis of the state" (the tendency for government expenses to outrace revenues).

4. By using the rationale of "global competition" to drive down the living standards of the majority, the corporate class has shifted more and more wealth from our pockets to theirs. This growing inequality is producing resentment and rebellion—here and abroad.

Yet counterposed to the relentless globalization of the economy is the globalization of grassroots democracy. Individuals and community groups are gradually building an alternative society guided by social justice and environmental sustainability rather than by greed. We conclude the book with an examination of these efforts.

Do We Want Just a Market, or a Just Market?

When the United States came out of World War II as the dominant industrial country, it was logical that the dollar would become the global currency, that U.S.-based corporations would dominate world markets, and that the U.S. would have the strongest hand in shaping global institutions such as the World Bank and the International Monetary Fund.

This dominance allowed U.S. transnational corporations to expand to gigantic proportions. Many of the Fortune 500 companies now have annual revenues larger than the gross national product of most Third World countries, and even larger than the GNP of industrial countries such as Finland, Denmark and Norway.[1]

The global reach of large corporations has disconnected them from national needs and desires. *Business Week* points out that "As cross-border trade and investment flows reach new heights, big global companies are effectively making decisions with little regard to national boundaries. Though few companies are totally untethered from their home countries, the trend toward a form of 'stateless' corporation is unmistakable."[2]

As corporations have developed the ability to tap into a huge global labor pool, they have less need for the social welfare policies of any particular nation. Global companies may want various kinds of *subsidies* from the government, but when it comes to government regulations that could allow the people to exert control over business, corporate ideology preaches free trade, deregulation and the downsizing of government. The possibility of truly democratic government is the most serious threat to the power of large corporations—so government must be dismantled!

With a global labor pool at their disposal, transnational corporations are less dependent on any particular national workforce. The first graph on the next page shows that in recent decades U.S. corporations have been cutting jobs here while expanding employment abroad. And the percentage of their total profits that derive from overseas operations has been rising sharply. (See second graph on following page.)

The old dictum, what's good for General Motors is good for the country, has a hollow ring in an age of globalization and corporate downsizing. After laying off more than 70,000 workers since 1993, General Motors now ranks as the wealthiest U.S. corporation, raking in more than $168 billion in revenues in 1995 alone—that's equal to the annual wages of more than 19 million Americans earning the minimum wage.

The increasing globalization of U.S. corporations gives them leverage to hold down wages and resist unionization. Average real wages (corrected for inflation) have been falling since the early 1970s. By 1992, average weekly earnings in the private, non-agricultural part of the U.S. economy were 19 percent below their peak in the early 1970s. Nearly one-fourth of the U.S. workforce now earns less than the 1968 minimum wage!

Job Loss/Gain in U.S. Multinational Corporations
(1983-1992)

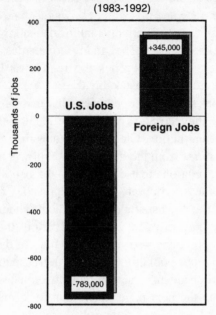

Percent of US Corporate Profits from U.S.-Owned Facilities Overseas

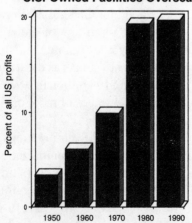

Source: *Corporate Power and the American Dream* (New York: The Labor Institute, 1995).

The trend toward less unionization is evident in the graph below, which shows a steady decline in union membership since the 1950s. This is a chicken-and-egg relationship because weaker unions are less able to restrict corporate behavior and the resulting freedom of action for global corporations means unions will be weakened further by companies putting their workers here in competition with low-paid workers abroad.

Working People Feel Insecure

The restructuring of our political and economic life due to globalization may be as significant a process as the industrial revolution. In early 1996 the mainstream media—incited by the rhetoric of Republican presidential candidate Pat Buchanan— focused an unusual amount of attention on the plight of U.S.

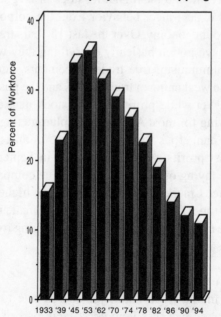

Unionization Rates for U.S. Private Sector Employees Are Dropping

Source: *Corporate Power and the American Dream* (New York: The Labor Institute, 1995).

workers in a globalizing economy.

As the *New York Times* editorialized on February 25, 1996: "Voters are clearly unnerved by corporate restructurings and the search for cheaper labor overseas." The *Times* went on to point out that "between 1991 and 1995, nearly 2.5 million Americans had lost their jobs because of corporate restructuring" and these job losses occurred "as the top pay for corporate executives has soared to nearly 200 times that of the average worker."

The February 26, 1996 issue of *Newsweek* ran a blaring cover story on corporate downsizing entitled "Corporate Killers." The piece was blunt in its criticism of corporate insensitivity: "Something is plain wrong when stock prices keep rising on Wall Street while Main Street is littered with the bodies of workers discarded by big companies like AT&T, Chase Manhattan and Scott Paper. Once upon a time, it was a mark of shame to fire your workers *en masse.* Today, the more people a company fires, the more Wall Street loves it, and the higher its stock price goes."

One would expect nicer behavior from the corporate chieftains who run our economy. Over the last 15 years transnational corporations have gotten basically everything they wanted: the collapse of communism, free trade agreements, deregulation, lower taxes, the weakening of trade unions and the pushing down of wage rates. Yet while profits and the stock market soar, the standard of living for most Americans is plummeting.

There is a dangerous dynamic at work. In an effort to cut costs and boost profits, AT&T announced in September 1995 that they were laying off 40,000 workers. The company's share price on the stock market immediately jumped higher. Because the salaries of top AT&T executives are partly made up of share ownership, the executives are personally benefiting from the suffering of thousands of dislocated families.

Technology Turned Against Us

Amid the media hype about job losses due to corporate downsizing, a key fact was ignored: a large part of the unemployment afflicting our country is due to a centuries-old drive by companies to replace workers with technology.

Top management sees technology as a way to dump workers—who make demands and question authority—and replace them with machines, which have not been known to form unions.

The trend is evident when you consider that employment in the U.S. manufacturing sector has declined over the past 30 years from 33 percent of the total workforce to less than 17 percent, even though our manufacturing sector has steadily increased output. As this trend continues we will see the elimination of most U.S. manufacturing jobs.

Contrary to what we've been told, the service sector (telecommunications, banking, insurance, real estate, retail and wholesale trade) will *not* replace the jobs lost in the manufacturing sector. First, the pay tends to be lower in the service sector. Second, technology is also replacing workers in the service sector. Whole layers of white collar office workers are being replaced by small, highly skilled teams using the latest computer technology. Thousands of postal workers have been made redundant by optical scanners and computerization. Between 1983 and 1993 banks in the United States replaced 179,000 human tellers with automated teller machines, and even more bank employees will be cut in years to come.

It's not that technology is necessarily bad, but when technological innovation is used to get rid of workers, with no systematic program to create meaningful replacement jobs, the result is widespread insecurity that saps worker morale. Is it just a coincidence that the U.S. Postal Service has imposed years of high-tech speedup on its workers—thus boosting profits to record levels—and is also notorious for its workers being among the most severely alienated in the world?

Our government hides unemployment by defining it away. The common sense definition of unemployment—people wanting a job but unable to get one—puts the number of unemployed in 1994 at 15.9 million, or 12.5 percent of the workforce. The official rate (6.1 percent in 1994) is reached by not counting the 6 million workers who want jobs but are so discouraged they've stopped looking, and counts as fully employed some 30 million who are only working part-time.[3]

Although employers may no longer need us as workers, they *do* need us as consumers. As a recently laid-off veteran of Bendix Corporation put it: "If they had their way, management would have robots doing everything in the plant, but they forget that robots don't buy anything."[4]

If each individual corporation stays focused on climbing the profit ladder in an increasingly global marketplace, it will shed workers for any reason that makes the company more profitable. At the micro-economic level of the company this makes sense. But when all these micro-economic decisions to cut workers are added up, the macro-economic impact is stagnation and all the social ills that go with it.

The Casino Economy

Another key dynamic of the globalized economy is the massive shift of capital from productive investment in the "real economy" to speculative investment in the "casino economy."

It's quite logical. If you have a few million dollars to invest, there are two basic approaches to choose from. You can invest in the real economy by building a factory to make bread or shoes or some other product or service that meets a human need; or you can invest your money in paper assets: stocks, bonds, mutual funds or a wide range of financial instruments that may not create many jobs or useful products but they do pay you a good rate of interest without all the bother of investing directly in production. Also, these speculative investments tend to be more liquid (able to be converted to cash) than investments in the real economy.

In recent years we have seen explosive growth in a new form of financial speculation: the "derivatives" market that is even one more step removed from the real economy. These investments 'derive' their value from underlying assets such as stocks, bonds or currencies, but they are merely bets as to whether the value of the underlying asset will rise or fall over a given period of time. So you might bet that the Japanese *yen* will fall in value over the next 6 months relative to Thailand's currency, the *bhat*. There are an endless variety of derivatives, designed merely to help investors hedge against risk, *not* to produce anything real.

To see how important the derivatives market has become, compare it to global trade in real goods. The annual value of global merchandise trade is about $4 trillion. The global derivatives market equals this dollar volume of transactions in about two days!

The globalization of capital markets and the shift of investments from the real economy to the casino economy has weakened the power of government to control national economies and protect people's jobs. Washington and other national governments are held hostage by the mobility of globalized capital. Companies can threaten to move out when confronted with higher taxes or stiffer regulations.

Bankrupting Our Government

As fewer workers are gainfully employed, income tax revenue to the government dries up at the same time as the demand for government services such as unemployment insurance and food stamps increases.

The squeeze between declining government income and increasing government expenses has produced record budget deficits and an expanding mountain of government debt. Federal government debt stood at $4.9 trillion in early 1996. The interest we pay to the owners of that debt ($232 billion in 1995) is now one of our largest federal budget expenditures: without this expenditure, there would be *no* budget deficit.

In the heated debate over the federal budget, Congress and the media have focused our attention on the *spending* side of the ledger. But the other side—revenue coming into the government—is just as important. Conservatives have convinced many Americans that excessive spending on social programs is the key reason for the fiscal crisis of the state. Yet a more crucial problem is that the wealthy corporations dominating our government are able to avoid paying their fair share of taxes.

Both major political parties are uncritical supporters of the "free market" and globalization of the economy. Yet this very process of increasing economic gigantism is behind the budget crisis and the long-term insolvency of our government. As corporations have grown in size they have expanded their capacity for lobbying our elected leaders to reduce corporate taxes and remove restrictions on the international movement of commodities and money. Plus, innovations in computers and telecommunications allow financiers to move billions of dollars around the world instantly, making it more difficult for governments to monitor and tax international transactions.

As the corporate share of the tax load was cut, who picked up the slack? A big portion was shifted to working people. In the early 1950s, corporations paid 76 cents in taxes for every one dollar paid by families and individuals. By 1992 corporations were paying just 21 cents for every one dollar in taxes paid by families and individuals. (See graph on the following page.)

The World's Biggest Debtor

Not *all* of the tax load could be pushed onto the current generation of workers. Some of it was financed through deficit spending: issuing government bonds to borrow from the capital markets—in other words, taxing our children and grandchildren.

It is odd that the Republicans have made a big issue of the deficit and the national debt, seeing as it was Republican presidents (Reagan and Bush) who created the record deficits that produced most of the national debt. When Ronald Reagan took office on January 20, 1981 the national debt was under $1 trillion. By the end of the Bush administration, on January 20, 1993, the national debt had quadrupled to $4 trillion. The interest we taxpayers fork over to bondholders on this additional $3 trillion in debt (figuring at an average of 7 percent) comes to $210 billion: far more than the current budget deficit of $172 billion. If Reagan and Bush hadn't splurged on the military while giving huge tax breaks to their corporate backers, there would be no budget deficit in 1996.[5]

As economists of all political stripes have noted, government debt is not necessarily bad if it is invested in things such as education or infrastructure which add to the productive potential of the nation. But when the debt is squandered on the military or on corporate welfare, its main impact is to make our society more unequal.

One of the long-term effects of budget deficits and skyrocketing debt is a large transfer of wealth upward in the class structure of our country. During the 1980s, U.S. taxpayers transferred $1.1 trillion in interest payments to the wealthy corporations and indi-

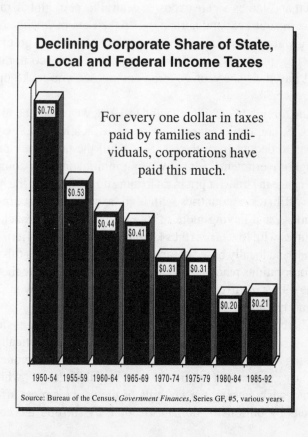

Declining Corporate Share of State, Local and Federal Income Taxes

For every one dollar in taxes paid by families and individuals, corporations have paid this much.

1950-54	1955-59	1960-64	1965-69	1970-74	1975-79	1980-84	1985-92
$0.76	$0.53	$0.44	$0.41	$0.31	$0.31	$0.20	$0.21

Source: Bureau of the Census, *Government Finances*, Series GF, #5, various years.

viduals who own the national debt. In the 1990s some $2 trillion will be redistributed upward on the social ladder via interest payments on the national debt.[6]

Who Pays, Who Benefits?

A key trend in the United States is that working people increasingly pay the costs of government, yet government increasingly serves business interests. Because big corporations have far more influence over politicians than we do, they have been able to cut their taxes while pressuring government to increase corporate welfare.

In their book, *America: Who Really Pays the Taxes?*, Donald Barlett and James Steele expose a central facet of globalization. "As companies expand abroad, so do their tax payments to foreign governments. And as the taxes they pay abroad go up, the taxes they pay to the U.S. Treasury go down. When corporations don't pay their share of government's costs, you make up the difference."[7]

The foreign tax credit, enacted in 1918, was designed to support U.S. companies expanding overseas: it allows U.S. corporations to deduct from their U.S. tax bill the taxes they pay to foreign governments. Plus, by being multinational, a company can engage in "transfer pricing": loading up expenses on the books of its affiliates in countries with high taxes (thereby getting deductions), and having more of its profits accrue to branches in countries with low taxes (thus keeping more of the profits). Individuals and locally based companies cannot avoid taxes this way. "If corporations paid taxes in the 1990s at the same rate they did in the 1950s, nearly two-thirds of the federal deficit would disappear overnight."[8]

There are two other key ways the tax load gets transferred from the wealthy to the rest of us. "First, by dramatically increasing Social Security tax rates and then using the money for ordinary government programs—not Social Security—while simultaneously cutting the tax bills of the nation's most affluent citizens by billions of dollars. Second, by shifting the cost of billions of dollars in programs once underwritten by the federal government to state and local governments, whose tax systems impose a much heavier burden on people in the middle and at the bottom." [9] The mixing of trust fund accounts such as Social Security with general revenue was started during the Vietnam War: it reduced the deficit by billions and helped cover up the real cost of the war.

Barlett and Steele sum up the impact of globalization on our tax system: "As the global economy grows, so, too, will your taxes, as the overall burden continues to be transferred from large corporations to small and medium-sized businesses and middle-income taxpayers." [10]

Corporate Welfare

Despite the failure of corporations to carry their fair share of the tax load, they get generous corporate welfare totalling more than $167 billion per year—more than three times what we spend on all programs usually described as 'welfare' such as housing assistance, food stamps and Aid to Families with Dependent Children. [11] Corporate welfare comes in many forms.

• *Tax reform*: According to the Congressional Budget Office, special business-tax provisions cost the federal government nearly $70 billion per year. Just one tax law, the 1986 Tax Reform Act, by 1994 had cost the taxpayers some $200 billion in tax cuts for the wealthiest one-fifth of one percent of the U.S. population. [12]

• *The Pentagon*: By purchasing weapons, food and many other products, the Pentagon's $265 billion annual budget is a huge subsidy to corporations. How much less profitable would our electronics industry and our nuclear power industry be without large military expenditures? [13]

• *Agribusiness*: Every year tens of billions of tax dollars go to agribusiness. Because the payments are based on size of output, the top 1 percent of producers get as much as the bottom 80 percent. Plus, large corporations get federal money to push exports: Pillsbury got $2.9 million to promote its pies and muffins abroad; Sunkist got $10 million to push its oranges; Cargill, with a net worth of $3.6 billion, has received $1.29 billion in subsidies since 1985.[14]

• *Timber industry*: In 1994, Washington spent $140 million building roads in national forests, mainly to help timber companies harvest our trees.

The hypocrisy of the welfare debate was summarized this way by *Business Week* : "A GOP that believes social welfare breeds personal dependency can't go on pretending that corporate welfare builds a strong economy."[15]

Is the U.S. Becoming a Third World Country?

Where will these main features of globalization—U.S. companies moving jobs abroad, thousands of workers being replaced by technology, the weakening of the U.S. trade union movement, changes in tax legislation to favor wealthier taxpayers—lead us? *Business Week* reports: "The gap between high- and low-income families has widened steadily since about 1980, hitting a new high every year since 1985."[16]

Despite what politicians say, 'growth' is making things worse, not better. "Between 1977 and 1989 the one percent of families with incomes over $350,000 received 72 percent of the country's income gains while the bottom 60 percent lost ground."[17]

A key reason for the decline in the majority's income share has been the steady fall in real wages. In 1992, average weekly earnings in the private, non-agricultural part of the U.S. economy were 19 percent below their peak in the early 1970s. Nearly one-fourth of the U.S. workforce now earns less in real terms than the 1968 minimum wage! Add another 5-10 percent of the population who have no jobs at all, and you've got a significant portion of the population living in poverty. Hence, *Newsweek*'s conclusion that "millions of Americans believe they're being screwed by corporate America and Wall Street."[18]

Corporate profits and the salaries of top management have soared. Corporate profits are up 40 percent since 1993, and, as *Business Week* reported, the average pay of Chief Executive Officers at the 362 largest companies in the U.S. jumped 30 percent during 1995 to an average of $3,746,392.[19]

The sharp growth in inequality caused U.S. Secretary of Labor Robert Reich to warn: "We have the most unequal distribution of income of any industrial nation in the world ... we can't be a prosperous or stable society with a huge gap between the very rich and everyone else."

But data on *income* is not the best indicator of inequality. Wealth measured by ownership—stocks, bonds, savings accounts, real estate—is a far better measure of real power in society. As the pie charts on the following page reveal, the ownership of property such as stocks, bonds and real estate in the United States is extremely unequal. Yes, millions of Americans own some stock, but the overwhelming majority of the stock (81.2%) is held by just ten percent of the population.

A 1995 study by the Twentieth Century Fund shows that since the late 1970s wealth inequality in the U.S. has been increasing. By the 1990s, the richest one percent of Americans owned *twice* as much wealth as the poorest 80 percent![20]

Contrary to what the Republicans have been preaching, it is *not* big government that is undermining Mainstreet, USA. Rather, mainstreet is being undermined by the fact that our government is dominated by monied interests—and those monied interests are increasingly global, owing no allegiance to any particular country. What can we do about this predicament? Plenty!

A Need for Unity

The latter section of this book contains numerous examples of ways people are organizing to resist top-down globalization and build alternative institutions. There are hundreds of organizations doing anti-systemic work but they are not united in a coordinated effort. By getting acquainted with the different types of organizing going on, we can take steps toward unifying the movement for change.

The chapters in the final section of the book are not exhaustive: they aim merely to acquaint the reader with a range of options and introduce some of the more interesting tactics for re-

U.S Wealth Distribution Is Very Unequal

Real Estate Ownership
(excluding main residence)

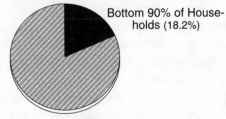

Bottom 90% of House-
holds (18.2%)

Top 10% of Households (81.8%)

Stock Ownership

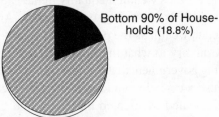

Bottom 90% of House-
holds (18.8%)

Top 10% of Households (81.2%)

Bond Ownership

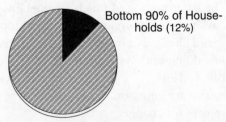

Bottom 90% of House-
holds (12%)

Top 10% of Households (88%)

Source: Federal Reserve Bank data in *Left Business Observer*, #72, April 3, 1996, p.5.

sisting corporate domination and developing alternative institutions.

In the Conclusion we lay out major areas of reform work and list the names and phone numbers of organizations we feel are doing exemplary work. No amount of facts or good analysis will fix what's wrong with the system, only organizing can do that.

Section 1

Corporate Power and the Global Economy

We live in a time when the power to shape the way we live and think is increasingly concentrated in the hands of a few hundred large, global corporations. Despite the growing influence of these institutions, the average person on the street knows little about them. Yet popular distrust of the corporate behemoths is spreading.

What are the basic dynamics of corporate globalization and the significance of corporate power for our quality of life? In "Stateless Corporations: Lords of the Global Economy," Richard Barnet gets to the heart of why we should be concerned about global corporations having so much power over our lives. In "Giants Stalk, Creation Trembles," Kirkpatrick Sale exposes the "gospel of globalism" and its main trends (monoculturalism, technophilia, consumptivitis and giantism). David Korten ("When Corporations Rule the World") examines how our belief in government of, by and for the people has been pushed aside by a global economic system in which government policy is dominated by the corporate bottom line—maximizing profits. In "Rules of the Game," Jerry Mander lays out eight mandates that the global economy imposes on corporate conduct. Russell Mokhiber's "Corporate Crime: Underworld U.S.A.," exposes how corporate crime costs our society more than all street crime combined, yet gets almost no media coverage and very little punishment from the justice system. Ralph Nader, in "Billions for Corporations, Bills for the People," concludes the section by showing just how much the executive branch of our government is dominated by corporate interests. He also lays out specific policies that could help citizens regain control of our society.

1

Stateless Corporations:

Lords of the Global Economy

Richard J. Barnet

It is seldom noted in the mainstream press that the world's 358 billionaires have a combined net worth of $760 billion, equal to that of the bottom 45 percent of the world population; or that the average C.E.O. in the United States now brings home about 149 times the average factory worker's pay; or that in recent years an estimated 18 percent of American workers with full-time jobs earned poverty-level wages; or that every other black baby in America is born into a family living below the poverty line; or that, since 1973, the number of American children living in poverty has increased by 50 percent, so that 22 percent now grow up poor, and the number keeps increasing.

Despite such statistics and many more like them, it remains an article of faith among most politicians and in boardrooms that what is good for General Motors is still good for America. Yet global corporations chartered in Delaware and flying the American flag now see themselves, even advertise themselves, as "stateless." Corporate executives disavow any special relationship to the United States or to its people. As Martin Davis, former chairman of Paramount Communications, put it, "You can't be emotionally bound to any particular asset." As mega-companies search the world for bargain labor, sell their stock on exchanges from London to Hong Kong and pin more and more of their hopes on customers in the emerging markets, most of them in Asia, they are walking away from the enormous public problems their private decisions create for American society.

At the same time, the influence of business giants over the daily lives of Americans is growing as ownership of the media is concentrated in fewer and fewer corporations, while big money plays an ever more decisive role in the political process. With the continuing decline of unions in the private sector, widespread disillusionment with government and the resurrection of unfettered free-market ideology, transnational corporations now exercise more power over the U.S. political system than at any time since the early decades of this century.

Because of the growth of corporate power, the accountability of private enterprises to workers, managers and the communities where they operate has declined markedly in the past twenty years. More than a quarter of the world's economic activity now comes from the 200 largest corporations. Up to one-third of world trade takes place among different units of a single global company. This means that prices are set, not by the mystical forces of the free market, but by corporate administrators who can arrange to have profits show up in tax havens and accomplish other miracles of creative accounting that improve the global bottom line.

The consequences of these developments are a shrinking tax base, accelerated joblessness, mounting insecurity in the workplace, increasing poverty and an ideological climate in which the breathtaking inequality between the highly publicized super-rich and the growing army of the poor rarely makes it onto the political screen. By taking advantage of an expanding global menu of profitable opportunities, U.S. corporations have reinvented themselves and in the process profoundly changed their relationship to American society.

From 1950 to the mid-1970s, the interests of large, U.S.-based corporations coincided in important ways with the interests of large numbers of Americans. In those high-growth years, thanks largely to strong unions and an activist government supported by both parties, big companies created tens of millions of well-paid jobs, provided health care and pensions, and brought women and minorities into the work force. The 1950s were scarcely a golden age of democracy, but corporations played a positive role in a number of important ways. The sustained industrial boom after World War II opened a window for blacks from the South to migrate to the factories of the North. Thousands made it into the blue-collar ranks, and their children entered the middle class in growing numbers. By the end of the 1980s, the percentage of African-Americans in the middle class, never more than 5 percent in the pre-civil rights era, was over 25 percent. Women's horizons expanded in the postwar prosperity, and so in time did their opportunities in the marketplace.

In major industries across the country, corporations facing powerful unions purchased peace in the workplace with high wages and generous benefits; they passed on the cost to the consumer, but in the process they ushered in a new middle class that could buy a home and two cars on credit. Companies like I.B.M. became private welfare states, offering secure lifetime employment and pensions that both managers and workers could count on. Thanks to the new prosperity and more equitable income distribution, median family income tripled between 1950 and 1970.

The global job crisis of the 1990s results from the interactions of the dramatic advances in labor-saving technologies and the equally remarkable expansion of the international labor market. "Competitiveness" is the mantra of this new economy, and the winning strategies involve "downsizing" labor costs and increasing market power through corporate takeovers. A global pool of bargain labor is available to companies making virtually anything and, increasingly, to corporations selling insurance, data of every description and legal, engineering and accounting services. About a third of the jobs in the United States are at risk to the growing productivity of low-wage workers in China, India, Mexico and elsewhere, and this new reality exerts downward pressure on wages and working conditions for millions of Americans who still hold jobs. Because corporations now control the technology to shift operations anywhere, the strike threat is rarely an effective instrument of collective bargaining. Management now wields the more credible threat: Take it or we leave.

The proportion of the U.S. work force in private industry organized for collective bargaining—now under 12 percent— is smaller than it was in 1936, the year after enactment of the Wagner Act, the principal New Deal labor law reform. The decline of Big Labor's political clout is reflected in changing governmental attitudes toward workers' rights. In the Reagan/ Bush years, widespread retaliation against organizing activities took place while the National Labor Relations Board looked the other way. The board is now more conscientious, but most unionbusting activities—such as the permanent replacement of striking workers—are within the law, and the unions' efforts to stop the erosion of their bargaining power went nowhere even when Democrats controlled Congress. Given the mood of the new G.O.P. majorities in the House and Senate, corporations will be even freer to shift production to areas where workers are willing to settle for lower pay and fewer benefits.

As technology eliminates all sorts of routine jobs, the number of "superstar" or "winner take all" jobs, as some economists call them, has jumped spectacularly, even though they make up a tiny fraction of the work force. C.E.O.s with multimillion-dollar salaries, virtuoso deal-makers, star lawyers, anesthesiologists, TV faces and pop musicians whose talent, connections or luck have propelled them to the top of their profession bring home a fortune every year even as the median earnings of the professional class and most entertainers stay flat. Stanford economist Paul Krugman notes that between the late 1970s and the early 1990s "the real wages of low-ranked workers like janitors fell 15 percent or more, while the real earnings of high-end occupations like doctors and corporate executives rose 50 percent or more."

The great financial houses, insurance companies and real estate firms, touted in the early 1980s as the post-industrial job machine that would take care of the people who were losing their jobs to robots or to corporate flight, provide low-paid and increasingly insecure employment. Political analyst Edward Luttwak calculated that, in 1992, the 4.9 million non-supervisory employees in these industries were making an average hourly wage of $10.14—less than the average production worker, and considerably less than is needed to raise a middle-class family in global financial capitals like Manhattan or San Francisco. The 1.1 million bank tellers and clerks earned $8.19 an hour, while the 48,500 back-office employees in brokerage houses earned an average salary of $28,142 a year. Middle managers are also casualties of corporate restructuring. The median earnings of the 2 million American men between 45 and 54 with four years of college (all but 150,000 of them white) fell in constant dollars from $55,000 in 1972 to $41,898 in 1992.

This pressure on wages and salaries is only increased by the growing lust for downsizing. In the three years ending in March 1994, five companies—IBM, A.T.& T., GM, Sears Roebuck and G.T.E.—announced layoffs totaling 324,650 employees. An American Management Association study based on interviews with corporate executives concluded that payroll-trimming is now a permanent strategy for many companies. Even an occasional C.E.O. is sacrificed in the effort to get the corporation down to fighting trim. But most executives are too politically astute to let this happen, even when their performance sags. Over the past three years, Disney's Michael Eisner earned $215,911,000 in salary, bonuses and the exercise of stock options; Anthony O'Reilley of H. J. Heinz took home $114,177,000 in the same period. Neither Euro Disney gate receipts nor ketchup sales nor the stock performance of either company would appear to warrant such princely emoluments, as *Business Week* suggested when naming both C.E.O.s to its select list of "those who gave shareholders the least."

Job-slashers tend to be well rewarded. According to a study done by my colleagues Sarah Anderson and John Cavanagh, the C.E.O.s of twenty-three of the nation's twenty-seven top job-destroyers received raises last year averaging 30 percent (the figure does not include stock options in excess of $1 million, which most have). The irrelevance of poor corporate performance in setting executive compensation prompted Congress to make a gesture of disapproval. The Omnibus Budget Reconciliation Act of 1993 disallows tax deductions for executive remuneration in excess of $1 million. But this provision has a comfortable escape clause that exempts "performance-based compensation," that is, additional money or stock awarded an executive for meeting "performance goals" set by the corporation and approved by a compensation committee of outside directors. Since productivity growth and increased cash flow are primary corporate goals, this reform has the unintended effect of rewarding top executives for firing employees at every level but their own.

According to a 1993 study by the General Accounting Office [a research arm of Congress], more than 40 percent of corporations doing business in the United States with assets of $250 million or more "either paid no income taxes or paid income taxes of less than $100,000." In the 1950s, corporations operating in the United States paid 23 percent of all federal income taxes. By 1991, it was down to 9.2 percent, while the corporate share of state and local taxes stayed about what it was in 1965. The many opportunities open to corporations and wealthy stockholders to avoid taxes are not only creating a fiscal crisis for cities and states across the nation but making the tax burden of the much-courted but much-abused middle class even heavier; states and localities seek to extract revenue in small bites from consumers and modest homeowners through regressive sales and property taxes. These states and municipalities are so desperate for decent jobs that they bid against one another in offering subsidies to bring in plants. In one such deal, Alabama gave Mercedes-Benz a $253 million package, about $170,000 per job. Illinois gave Sears a $240 million tract of land just to stay put, but this did not prevent large Sears lay-offs throughout the state.

Even in states like California, with a well-organized revolt against local taxation, the tax burden increases while the services that such revenues are supposed to underwrite continue to decline. The drying up of public moneys means that for those who must depend on inadequate and demoralized public education, a national postal service that loses mail and is overburdened, and unresponsive police forces, living in America is an increasingly different experience from what it is for those who can afford private schools, Federal Express, security guards and other amenities provided by the great growth industry of the nineties, the privatization of public services.

More and more Americans now fear they will lose their job and the anchor it represents. Pensions are dangerously underfunded. G.M., for example, had an estimated $14 billion in unfunded pension liabilities in 1994. As a result, workers are increasingly expected to provide for their own retirement, sometimes with modest matching corporate contributions, often without. For millions of individuals who once had the expectation of lifetime employment and for communities with expectations of a secure economic base, what is disappearing is not just an income and lifestyle but trust in the corporation, a basic American institution that for years provided security and a sense of self-worth and purpose for millions of people.

Good news for people is bad news for corporate investors. When employment goes up the stock market tends to go down, because of fears of inflation. The link between unemployment and increased family stress, child abuse, alcoholism, suicide and mental illness has been well documented in many studies. This lack of security is undermining a whole set of beliefs and expectations about opportunity, equality and community on which democratic hopes are based. For those at the bottom of our society—especially young African-American men facing unemployment rates of 65 percent or more in major American cities—the prospect, as Cornel West has put it, is for lives of "horrifying meaninglessness, hopelessness, and (most important) lovelessness." The social costs, not to mention the uncalculated economic costs, of nihilistic rage are evident in our exploding inner cities.

That rage and the fury found almost everywhere else in the country is directed almost exclusively at government because the mainstream media virtually never target global corporations as major contributors to the nation's socio-economic woes, and because even if they did, the business behemoths would seem beyond reach. You can send a message by voting out an incumbent, but sending a message that corporate bureaucracies will hear takes considerably more money, time and patience.

Citizens' movements have scored victories in the struggle to reform corporate behavior with respect to auto safety and some environmental and health issues, but these successes have taken enormous effort and the dedication of a few people. Even so, most Americans feel powerless to change institutions that are putting people last, and the more overwhelmed they feel, the more corporate power grows. Yet the implacable logic of accelerating workplace insecurity, and the social crisis it clearly implies, is not on the agenda of either the Democrats or the Republicans. Neither party is prepared to take on the core political issue that is transforming American life, because both depend on corporate money and connections to win votes in the obscenely expensive, never-ending campaign that now defines American politics.

2

Giants Stalk, Creation Trembles

Kirkpatrick Sale

I t is not so surprising that the global corporations that stand to benefit from it have spent so much time and money trumpeting the virtues of what is described as the 'transnational economy' of the twenty-first century. What is far more surprising is that they've been allowed to get away with it so neatly, without more than a choir-stall of voices raised in dissent.

Of course it's true that the globalists have been able to develop a gospel full of such chapter and verse as 'efficiency', 'progress', 'individualism', 'productivity' and 'growth'—and those are hard canons to go up against. But a gospel, after all, is nothing more than a good story (Old English 'god'—good, plus 'spell'—tale). You would have thought that these days no one would be allowed to go around spinning their self-serving yarns without some sort of challenge.

Yet here we are with the global gospel everywhere triumphant. President Clinton (insofar as he has any convictions of his own) is a proclaimed internationalist, as are his Secretaries of Treasury, Commerce and Energy. And the chief futurist on his team, Labor Secretary Robert Reich, has been known primarily for his embrace of a global economy in which the U.S. attracts multinational investment by specializing in high-tech/high-intellect production. The Uruguay round of GATT and the new North American Free Trade Agreement, after they went through some tinkering to satisfy a few protectionist types, ratified the globalism of the industrial world. And the World Bank, IMF, Group of Seven, the European Economic Union and the newly

Western-bought UN are in place to guide and protect it. No government anywhere seems inclined to try to halt this economic juggernaut.

And a juggernaut it is: in truth, a Second Industrial Revolution at work. "Broad, global forces for change," in the words of historian Paul Kennedy, "are bearing down upon humankind in both rich and poor societies alike." These include, he says, sweeping technological changes in production and marketing, a 24-hour-a-day worldwide financial trading system, an unfettered relocation of factories and trading of products across national borders. "Every country is challenged by these global forces for change," he says. Most of them, especially in the South, will fail to meet that challenge.

Well, if things are bearing down on us like that, I think it behooves us to take some account of the gospel they are riding on and the values—so deeply held that they are not usually even perceived as arguable—behind it. If those values are allowed to go unchallenged and unaltered, and the gospel of globalism does indeed triumph, the result cannot be anything but the increasing impoverishment of the South, dangerous economic and political distentions for the North and environmental ruin for the greater part of the earth.

In one sense the values of globalism are just the values of modernism—the overarching ideology of industrial capitalism—writ large. There are four key values that are central to the emerging global order and are also vulnerable to examination.

• **Monoculturalism** — The idea that the world is a single, interdependent market lies behind the commitment to free trade and what the Chief Executive Officer of United Technologies calls "a worldwide business environment unfettered by government interference." In this industrial monoculture factories and people, like parts, are interchangeable, and 'Coca-Colonization' extends to every corner of the globe.

The first victims are of course the familiar nation-states, whose borders and governments are now impediments, as much in the

North where administrations are seduced or bought, as in the South where they are subverted or controlled. Thus over the last decade we have seen the disintegration of national governments in Eurasia, the total collapse of central authority in a variety of states and a hell-bent drive to join in the capitalist game from China and Vietnam to Poland and East Germany.

But monoculturalism won't stop there. Its need, which has always been the need of industrial capital, is to destroy regional identities, indigenous cultures and even stable communities. Traditions rooted there—self-sufficiency, sustainability, handicrafts, 'enoughness'—must be eliminated for the market system to succeed.

• **Technophilia** — What was once a simple drive to replace human work by mechanical work has become a near obsession in our machine-dominated society. It is not merely that the globalists have machines that can slosh billions of dollars around the world instantly at the press of a key, or can equally alter genes or ecosystems or atmospheric layers. What's critical is that their perspectives must succumb to the patterns set by these machines. Problems must be posed in ways that can be solved by them.

There's a lot of talk these days about the 'information age' and a 'post-industrial world built on "knowledge industries" and the like. It is what America is supposed to become in the next century, along with a few other chosen partners like Japan and Germany, while most of the industrial world and all but a select few parts of the industrializing world drop farther into poverty. It sounds good to many, and even astute critics like David Morris of the Washington-based Institute for Self Reliance seem to believe that computers will empower individual citizens and permit decentralized independence from the megacorporations.

Nonsense. 'Information' is just the currency of the globalists' machines. The globalists made the machines in their own image and they control the kinds of information those machines are capable of using: the quantifications of life, the reduction of human complexities to analogues. And they are not much interested in empowering citizens or they wouldn't give us those machines in the first place. To believe otherwise is to fall into the trap of technophilia: a velvet-lined trap, with its VCRs and microwaves and wordprocessors, but a terrible snare and delusion nonetheless.

There should be no doubt about the fundamental dangers of believing that machines are here to solve our problems. They exist out of their own imperative, a technological imperative backed by a utilitarian science that, as Lewis Mumford so cogently saw, is really 'the ultimate religion of our seemingly rational age'. He called it 'the Myth of the Machine' and warned explicitly of what it meant: 'bigger and bigger, more and more, farther and farther, faster and faster'—not to mention worse and worse, riskier and riskier, deadlier and deadlier.

There should also be no doubt that if there is to be any salvation for the twenty-first century it will come through biophilia, some kind of profound and thorough-going love of nature and a respect for her laws and imperatives. All of which, I need hardly say, are opposed to those of globalism.

• **Consumptivitis** — It is so elemental that we almost overlook it, but the unalterable foundation of industrialism is the disease of unending consumption—of what, it hardly matters—and its accompanying unlimited production. A global economy guided by free trade—that is free of environmental laws and price constraints and resource allotments and national allegiances and labour restrictions—can go into a frenzy of production and consumption, prodded by advertising, sanctioned by consumer culture and driven by the materialism that lies at the heart of Western society.

This consumption need not be equal, within or among nations, to work. In fact the accumulated buying power of the rich must come from the increasing impoverishment of the poor: the underclasses within industrial society (growing by record numbers in the 1980s and 1990s) and the still-colonized countries elsewhere, whose distance from the rich nations is vast and growing wider each year.

There are limits to all this, of course, and they are set by the earth and its systems, already seriously over-stressed. But they are of no concern to globalists, since by definition they have no home and couldn't care less about that care-of-home that goes by the name 'ecology'. Without restraints the megacorporations are free to use up resources at an ever-faster rate (remember, the scarcer the resource the more valuable it becomes), to foul the biosphere in their processing of them and to poison air and soil in their disposal of them. There is no concern for the inevitable ecocidal end of this because the corporation, again by definition, does not comprehend the future and must maximize profits in the shortest run possible.

• **Giantism** — Perils there may be in bigness, as the struggling IBM, General Motors and even Mitsubishi demonstrate. But this is the imperative of successful globalism. What you lose now in workforce you simply gain later in hassle-free automation, reduced labor costs and increased profits. Despite its problems General Motors is still the number one American corporation. Moreover the occasional and inevitable misstep (for with all their megamachines, large enterprises are always less efficient than small) is more than made up for by the immense power the global players have. They can twist laws and regulations, shift plants around the globe, open or close markets, set prices, monopolize research and development. The rules, written by the big players, always favor the big players, and are designed to forgive them for their flaws and failures.

It has become commonplace to note that such power is beyond the control of any mere citizen or consumer. But corporations have never been democratic, nor were they ever meant to be. The largest of them are, for the most part, impervious not only to popular pressure but even to government suasion. They owe no loyalty to any town or even nation. Wasn't it revealing that the U.S. pavilion at the World's Fair in Spain in 1992 was such a meager, flimsy thing? The main reason was that American companies one after the other refused to kick in funds and thus become associated with the United States. They wished to be seen as 'global' instead.

And since there is no one to take them on and all the powerful international institutions like the World Bank are of their own making, there is no one to halt their increasing growth, or their increasing power to impoverish the people and imperil the earth. Giants really do stalk the world, and most of creation trembles.

The gospel of globalism made up of these essential values bids fair to sanction a corporatist catastrophe in this next century. And I'd be hard put to identify—alas, even to imagine—the forces that would be able to undermine its potent message and the likely outcome. We know what values we would put in its place: community, democracy, decentralization, biophilia, harmony, sustenance. But it is difficult to see what gospel would be able to proclaim them forcefully enough, effectively enough, quickly enough.

Perhaps there is comfort in the knowledge that, in time and probably not too far hence, the earth will recoil from the assault of globalism and in some awful spasm will dispel it and all its work, as a dog shakes off water after a plunge. Whether we will be here afterward, of course, is an open question.

3

When Corporations Rule the World

An Interview with David Korten

*W*hat do you mean when you write, *"Corporate institutions have emerged as the dominant governance institutions on the planet?"*

David Korten: In fact, the dominant governance system is the financial system, rather than the corporations themselves. The corporations are accountable to the globalized system of finance, which has transformed itself in very important and deeply troubling ways, and is now quite accurately described as a global gambling casino. This transformation grows out of a combination of the linking of all the world's financial markets into a single computerized system, and the fact that there have been major shifts in the way investment is done, particularly as mutual funds, pensions funds and trust funds have become much more dominant investment vehicles.

Today, when most people invest, very few buy shares in a company; instead, they buy shares in these funds, which are run by fund managers who are evaluated on the basis of very, very short-term results. The obvious example is the mutual funds whose results are published on a daily basis. It increasingly turns out that what we have referred to as investment is really a process of speculating, or betting, on very short-term price movements.

In a globalized system, where corporations are able to free themselves to a large extent from local regulation and any sense of community membership, they are increasingly accountable only to that global financial system. Managers are evaluated on the basis of their very short-term contributions to increases in share prices. That of course greatly constrains their perspective.

Over the last three years, the S&P 500 largest corporations have been increasing their profits by an average of 20 percent a year—and that begins to define the norm. It puts enormous pressure on corporate management to go for the short term. You do that by gobbling up more and more of the available market share, and passing more and more of your costs on to the community—by technological change to eliminate jobs, downgrade jobs, move jobs abroad to lower wage countries, by cutting corners on environmental regulations and by increasing the number of direct government subsidies through special tax breaks and handouts.

What does it mean to say that corporations are able to "hold public policy hostage?"

Korten: There are two pieces to that. First, as you erase national economic borders, and integrate national economies into a global economy in which companies are free to move their money and goods without restraint, the real competition is far less among firms—which are managing competition among themselves with mergers and acquisitions and strategic alliances. The real competition is among people and communities for a declining pool of jobs, and they compete by offering the lowest wages, the poorest working conditions and the least environmental restraint.

The other side of it is that corporations are putting enormous amounts of their money into buying politicians and rewriting legislation to serve their particular interests, to weaken environmental regulations, to weaken unions, to avoid any increases in minimum wages and to push through the trade agreements, which are really corporate bills of rights.

Do individual corporations have the ability to be different, to act more responsibly?

Korten: I think this goes to the heart of the problem. Unless a corporation is working in a particular niche situation, and is privately owned by a terribly socially conscious family or manager, it is virtually impossible to manage a corporation in a socially responsible way. Either it will be driven out of the market by competitors who are pursuing less responsible policies, or it will be bought by a corporate raider who sees the short-term profit in taking those actions. Or, as fund managers themselves become more active in the management affairs of corporations, the managers are likely to be replaced by shareholder action driven by fund managers.

Does that mean it is irrelevant whether or not a particular corporate executive is socially minded?

Korten: The critical thing that comes out here is that while business leaders have very little choice but to respond to the imperatives of the financial markets when playing within the system, they do not necessarily have to align with legislative agendas which are deeply contrary to the public interest in the pursuit of short-term corporate profits. Business people who are concerned about issues of social responsibility and the long-term viability of society can play a much larger role in insisting that their business colleagues not move us to the least possible regulation. They can do this by supporting appropriate legislation that will create a level playing field, but at a much higher level than now exists, meaning that all corporations will have to adhere to a higher level of social responsibility.

What are the strategic implications for citizen activists of the contention that corporate executives are themselves constrained in important ways?

Korten: Because of the systemic nature of the problem, the people who are engaged in campaigns against specific corporate wrongdoing in the end fight a losing battle. You can force some constraint through consumer boycotts or even embarrassment against a specific corporation on specific issues, but you are really fighting against the system, because the overall rewards to the corporation favor engaging in what should be considered corporate crime. We have to set our sights on changing the larger rules of the game.

My sense is that the basic direction in which we have to move is toward more localized economies, and breaking up massive concentrations of corporate power.

Why do you so strongly emphasize localism?

Korten: There are two large ways of describing it. One has to do with power and whether it is connected to a human interest or whether it is connected to a system of institutions that serve only the interests of the already economically powerful. If, as Adam Smith essentially recognized, you are dealing with a market system in which power is defined by money and control of productive assets, then the system is only likely to be equitable and tied to a larger public interest to the extent that ownership and power is very broadly distributed, rooted in people and basically by implication also rooted in community and a framework of community values.

When you get into a globalized economy, all of that stuff becomes detached. Ownership becomes delinked from community or workers. As the concentration of economic power grows greater and greater, the power to decide on resource allocation is concentrated in fewer and fewer hands that have special and unattached interests.

This leads back to the idea that, if you believe in democracy, you can't separate economic democracy and political democracy because of the extent to which political democracy gets bought out if you have enormous disparities in economic power. We therefore have to be very conscious of the conditions that sustain some degree of economic democracy. That comes back to equitable distribution and rooting economic power in sufficiently small units so that people can understand what is happening and can set local rules that are consistent with their values and circumstances.

Another way of posing this whole thing is to say that part of the reality of our modern world is that our lives are divided between two parallel realities. One is the world that is virtually defined by money and the institutions of money. The other is the living world, which is both a world of nature and people—the systems that sustain life.

The living world functions by a very different rhythm, a very different set of imperatives than the money world. For example, we have created money systems that have a growth imperative. This stems from the structuring of a money system that pays interest, thereby requiring economic expansion to pay the continuous rent on money, and from the dynamics of technological change and increasing productivity, which mean the economy must grow for any semblance of full employment to be maintained. In the living world, however, unrestrained growth is a sign of dysfunction; if individual organisms or species grow beyond their normal cycle, that is a dysfunction.

The more that the money world becomes globalized, the more the links between the living world and the money world become tenuous, and the more the money system predominates. To the extent that we bring the power and control back to the local level, so that the money system is embedded and controlled by people who are living normal lives, whose view of reality is not shaped entirely by the numbers they see on their computer screens as they trade shares, stock options and derivatives, you get a much greater likelihood that the decisions that we make in society will be consistent with living-world values.

Robert Reich, now U.S. Secretary of Labor, has argued that the nationality of a company is irrelevant from a public policy standpoint. What is your assessment of that claim?

Korten: At one level, he is absolutely right. The very term transnational means beyond nationality. Coca Cola, for example, recently announced it is reorganizing itself as a truly global company, in which North America is simply one division responsible for roughly a sixth of the corporation's business. These kinds of corporations clearly have very little sense of national identity or national interest. They couldn't care less about whether we have full employment in the United States, whether our education system works, whether our external payments are in balance or any of those sorts of things. At least it makes no more difference to them in the United States than it does in any other country. From that standpoint, if you are a community trying to negotiate with a corporation, the nationality is probably somewhat irrelevant, although I do believe the Japanese firms have some slightly greater sense of loyalty to Japan, although perhaps that is declining also.

Reich's argument is that this is a *fait accompli*. His answer is that we should educate everybody in the United States, so we can control all the symbol manipulator jobs in the world and outcompete everyone else and run the show.

In my view, that is naive—there is no way in the world we are going to capture all those jobs, nor that everyone who happens to be a U.S. citizen even necessarily has the potential to acquire the skills to be part of that class. It is also myopic, because it is part of a pattern of pitting the interests of one small group of people against the interests of all the rest. It is hard to see how that could ever make for a stable and peaceful, let alone just, world.

That is why we have to go beyond these kinds of solutions that take the status quo of a globalized economy dominated by transnational capital detached from human accountability as a *fait accompli*. We have to recognize that the globalized system was created through conscious choices and decisions. People had access to political power and used that access to change the rules in ways that served their particular interest, contrary to the larger public interest. If globalization is not a historical inevitability, but a matter of choice, then it is in our means to make different choices.

But that means that those choices are going to have to be made by a different group of people. This again brings us back to the importance of political reform, and the reclaiming of citizen sovereignty in democracy, getting big money out of politics and starting to design rules that work for people, including rules that localize markets, and localize economic power.

It is obviously not an easy agenda, and it is even harder to imagine it in the present political climate. But we are in a situation where the system is rapidly self-destructing, and the disillusionment with the political system is at an all-time high.

I do believe that awareness is building of the reasons why the system is malfunctioning. We need to advance that awareness building, and we also need to create awareness that there really are alternatives. We need to begin building credible alternative agendas that move us toward a very different political alignment, that combine the conservative values of community, individual responsibility and family with the liberal values of compassion, equity and international cooperation.

Do you think it is fair to characterize localism as a form of protectionism?

Korten: If protectionism is about giving preference to local employers who play by local rules, create local jobs, pay local taxes, function as members of the local community, then I don't have any problem with being a protectionist.

The anomaly here is that being a local protectionist is in many respects a far more internationally friendly posture than being an international competitor, in which you are trying to drive your rivals out of business and into destitution: that, to me, is the most internationally unfriendly posture.

All of this ties back to the issue of the real nature of the environmental problem, and the reality of environmental limits. Much of the impetus behind so-called free trade is to open up international borders in order to assure a small group of people free access to the world's remaining resources.

Part of moving toward more localized economies is to start asking questions of how can we maintain a decent, humane standard of living based on reliance on our own resources. This requires recognizing the traditional dynamic of colonialism, which was about getting a small group of people in the colonizing countries access to a large pool of wealth to support lifestyles that could not be supported purely on local resources. Globalization, and the ascension of corporate power, is an extension of that colonial process.

If you take gross figures of roughly 20 percent of the world's population consuming roughly 80 percent of the earth's resources, and you add the realization that we are now in many instances using the output of our natural systems at rates greater than can be sustained, you begin to see the real implications of our situation—there is no conceivable way that all of the world can be brought up to the levels of consumption of the high-consuming 20 percent. The earth's systems would simply collapse.

So we are really talking about issues of distribution and equity. And the more localized your economy, the more you are aware of the need for living within your local environmental means. In contrast, maintaining a global economy allows us to be far less aware of whose resources we are dependent on.

4

Corporate Rules of the Game

Jerry Mander

The corporate world is fortified by a complex web of factories, workers, machinery and money: all dedicated to producing a return on the investment of owners and stockholders. To reach that goal, all corporations share similar values and follow similar rules.

Rule #1 — Make a Buck

Corporations define success in two basic ways: the growth of assets and the rate of profit. These goals take precedence over concerns for the community or nation in which the corporation does business. There is a strong tension between the corporation's desire for profits and the demands of workers for a decent wage.

Rule #2 — Be Aggressive

Successfully climbing the corporate ladder means being aggressive and competitive. Colleagues compete fiercely with each other for promotions; workers are encouraged to compete with each other through special awards in order to increase productivity and profits. The Japanese labor-management approach of 'teamwork' in the plant merely shifts competition from individual workers to groups of workers. This urge to compete is now seen as basic human nature.

Rule #3 — Look After Number One

Decision-making within a corporation is ruled by the bottom

line. In practice this means the interests of the corporation and the interests of the community only overlap when it serves the corporation's purpose. A company may sponsor a baseball team, donate money to a hospital or underwrite a community orchestra, but corporate altruism is usually more public relations than community spirit. The fight to make corporations socially reponsible will always be an uphill battle since corporations are inherently selfish. Their essential responsibility is to their own financial survival, not to the welfare of the public.

Rule #4 — Follow Orders

The organizational structure of the corporate world is based on a strict pecking-order. There is a hierarchy of command and control that extends from the Board of Directors and Chief Executive Officer down to the lowliest workers at the bottom. Your place in the pecking-order determines your power, your rewards and your privileges. Orders flow from the top down as they do in other large institutions that use a strict hierarchy, such as the military and the government. Notions of hierarchy and status within the corporate world tend to reinforce the idea that inequality and conformity are natural: the world is made of leaders and followers and there is little we can do to change this fact of life.

Rule #5 — Embrace Technology

The modern corporation is both a creature and a captive of technology. Companies are engaged in a restless search for technological innovation to boost efficiency (i.e., increase revenue with less labor and capital). Thus all technology is considered benign and objective. In fact, modern technologies are biased toward the technocratic worldview that produces them. This view is based on linear thinking and a tendency to segment and quantify the world. Corporations are so fascinated by technology, they have no time for non-material values: Old-growth forests are so many board-feet of lumber; toxic wastes are subject to cost-benefit analysis; workers fighting for improved working conditions are threats to profitability.

Rule #6 — Join the Crowd

Corporations view the world as one big market: Social relationships are defined in terms of buying and selling, and human activity is seen as a straightforward battle to gain advantage over your neighbor. The result of this market vision is that human happiness and satisfaction are defined in terms of what we buy. Multinational corporations have been remarkably successful in spreading their attitudes and values around the globe. Television, advertising and films carry the corporate market view everywhere, steamrolling local culture in the process. This growing homogenization destroys opposition to the 'consumer society,' obliterates cultural diversity and accelerates the destruction of natural resources.

Rule #7 — Don't Look Back

Corporations have no allegiance to the present because they are riveted on the future and the need to grow. This consuming passion effectively removes them from the day-to-day concerns of the local community. With their eyes fixed firmly on tomorrow, corporations have little commitment to solving the mundane problems of everyday life. Staying flexible in order to be profitable means multinationals can and do pack up and move at the drop of a hat. Inside the corporation, life is highly-structured and geared to the clock. Yet corporations can be strangely ephemeral. The future is possibility; the present merely a viewpoint; and the past irrelevant—this operating principle undercuts the search for social stability.

Rule #8 — Neutralize Nature

Corporate activities and the natural world are fundamentally at odds. Manufacturing goods to be bought and sold in the marketplace is essentially a process of transforming raw materials extracted from nature into commodities. This exploitation of the environment is ingrained in corporate behavior: even service and financial corporations depend indirectly on the conquest of nature. As consumerism spreads around the globe, the search for raw materials accelerates and the ravaging of nature quickens. In an attempt to absorb criticism from environmentalists, multinationals have wrapped themselves in green rhetoric. Yet any serious attempt to challenge the underlying consumerist credo is still dismissed as subversive—which in essence it is.

How Do Corporations Maintain Access to Third World Markets?

Just about everyone knows that cigarette smoking causes cancer and other costly health side-effects. Yet governments that can ill afford these costs allow transnational corporations to peddle their deadly wares to the public. The following quote explains how it works.

"According to the World Health Organization (WHO), tobacco will kill some 10 million people per year by 2025—seven million of them in economically poor countries. Philip Morris, RJR Nabisco and B.A.T. are laying the groundwork for this health disaster by aggressively increasing their advertising, promotion, and influence-peddling in key expansion markets, such as Africa. In Africa, tobacco is as much an economic and environmental issue as a health issue. Tobacco transnationals have ensured access by offering African governments shares in their companies, providing senior management positions to people closely associated with officials in power, donating to projects supported by leading political figures, giving hand-outs to influential people, and winning support through economies which have become dependent on tobacco."

From INFACT Update, *Fall 1995. For information on INFACT's Campaign for Corporate Accountability, contact them at 256 Hanover St., Boston, MA 02113 (617) 742-4583.*

5

Corporate Crime: Underworld U.S.A.

Russell Mokhiber

No major political figure or publication has mustered the courage to address the country's current wave of corporate crime and violence, even though corporate crime inflicts far more damage on our society than all street crime combined.

How much damage corporations inflict is known only by the criminals, their highpowered lobbyists and their attorneys. (Robert Bennett, one of the nation's premier white-collar crime defense lawyers, has said that "90 percent of what I work on never sees the public light of day—and that should be true of any good white-collar crime defense attorney.")

Every year, the FBI issues its *Crime in the United States* report, which documents murder, robbery, assault, burglary and other street crimes. The report ignores corporate and white-collar crimes such as pollution, procurement fraud, financial fraud, public corruption and occupational homicide.

But some evidence indicates the scope of the problem. The FBI reports burglary and robbery combined cost the nation about $4 billion in 1995. In contrast, white-collar fraud, generally committed by intelligent people of means—such as doctors, lawyers, accountants and businessmen—costs an estimated 50 times as much—$200 billion a year, according to W. Steve Albrecht, a professor of accountancy at Brigham Young University.

The FBI puts the street homicide rate at about 24,000 a year. But the Labor Department reports that more than twice that number—56,000 Americans—die every year on the job or from occupational diseases such as black lung, brown lung asbestosis and various occupationally induced cancers.

Even these figures, which scarcely meet with any serious public attention or debate, don't get at the full scale of the problem. Most corporate wrong-doing and violence goes unreported for one compelling reason: unlike all other criminal groups in the United States, major corporations have enough power to define the law under which they live.

The auto industry is a case in point. Today, the federal auto safety law carries no criminal sanctions, thanks to the auto industry lobby. For years, auto safety advocates have sought to add criminal sanctions to the law, and for years, the auto lobby has blocked their passage.

This might seem to many mainstream observers as a harmless legislative perk. But consider that for more than 20 years the auto industry also defeated efforts to enact a federal law that would require air bags as standard equipment on all U.S. cars.

It wasn't that the industry didn't know how to save lives. General Motors produced more than 11,000 Chevrolets, Buicks, Oldsmobiles and Cadillacs with full front air bags in the early 1970s. Numerous studies predicted what the auto companies and safety experts are now seeing on the road: air bags are saving lives and preventing serious injury.

However, the industry didn't want to live under a life saving rule of law. So every time safety advocates brought the air bag law up in Congress, the crime lobby defeated it. It wasn't until 1991, after government procured cars demonstrated the lifesaving potential of air bags, that the industry gave in to growing public pressure.

Auto safety expert Byron Bloch, who owns an original production 1973 Chevy Impala with full front air bags, estimates that as many as 140,000 Americans—"almost three Vietnam walls worth of Americans"—have died in auto crashes since the early

1970s because the auto companies' legislative privilege effectively thwarted all efforts to develop and legally mandate the device in American cars.

Yet even if a genuine populist movement were to enact tough laws criminalizing the reckless conduct of corporations, there would still remain the problem of prosecution. And here, too, lurks a central, if unsurprising, obstacle to reining in corporate crime: Unlike most other criminal groups, corporations have enough power to influence prosecutors not to bring criminal charges.

According to former *New York Times* reporter David Burnham, all of the past half-dozen U.S. Attorneys General have publicly committed the Justice Department to a war against white-collar crime. But as Burnham reports in his book, *Above the Law: Secret Deals, Political Fixes and Other Misadventures of the U.S. Department of Justice*, the Department doesn't walk the talk.

Burnham—who now co-directs the Transactional Records Access Clearinghouse, which collects data on the performance of the U.S. government—finds that less than one half of one percent (250) of the criminal indictments (51,253) brought by the Department in 1994 involved environmental crimes, occupational safety and health crimes, and crimes involving product and consumer safety issues. Burnham doubts whether this record reflects the true level of corporate crime in America.

"In August 1993, the *National Law Journal* did a survey of general counsels of major corporations," Burnham told *Corporate Crime Reporter*. "Sixty-six percent of the counsels said they believed that their companies had violated federal or state environmental laws in the last year. You have tens of thousands of major corporations. You have a substantial number of the general counsels of these companies saying they are committing crimes. That speaks for itself."

Burnham believes that corporate criminals often get away because of "unacknowledged class biases, outright political deals, poorly drafted laws and incompetent investigators" at the Justice Department. When it comes to prosecuting white-collar crime cases, Burnham argues, "the Justice Department itself could be convicted of fraud."

On the job homicides are some of the most heinous crimes corporations could be charged with. Yet corporate violence that results in worker deaths rarely provokes criminal prosecutions, either at the state or federal level. The National Safety Council estimates that since the passage of the Occupational Safety and Health Act (OSHAct) in 1970, 250,000 workers have died on the job.

Many of these deaths stemmed directly from recklessness on the part of corporate employers, but according to the Occupational Safety and Health Administration (OSHA), only four people have done time for OSHAct violations.

Each year, OSHA refers only a handful of cases to the Justice Department for criminal prosecution. And Justice Department officials are reluctant to prosecute these cases, knowing that the federal workplace safety law allows for only six months in prison for a first offense.

This is a law enforcement obscenity. Harassing an animal gets you more jail time than criminal violations of the federal worker safety law. The maximum criminal penalty for harassing a wild burro on federal land is one year in jail, and seven people have been jailed for this crime.

Labor union activists have sought to strengthen the criminal provisions of the health and safety law over the years, but these efforts have been roundly defeated by big business interests in Congress. And the business-driven, anti-law enforcement climate in Washington often leaves OSHA pulling its punches in cases of the most egregious corporate conduct.

Take the case of Patrick Hayes. In October 1993, Hayes was smothered to death under 60 tons of corn at a Showell Farms, Inc. chicken-processing facility in De Funiak Springs, Florida. It took rescue workers five and a half hours to recover his body.

OSHA investigator Linda Campbell found six willful violations of the federal worker safety law and recommended a $530,000 fine against the company. Campbell also told Hayes' parents that she recommended a criminal prosecution of those responsible for Patrick's death.

But Campbell's superiors at OSHA overruled her determination, reducing the fines to $30,000 and downgrading the citations from "willful violations" to "serious." Because federal law requires a "willful violation" to prosecute a workplace death, this reversal blocked any possible federal criminal prosecution.

In cases like these, state officials should step into the breach and investigate the workplace death for a possible reckless homicide or manslaughter prosecution. When Ira Reiner was the Los Angeles County district attorney in the 1980s, he investigated every workplace death for a possible criminal prosecution—and took many of the cases to court.

One such prosecution is pending in Wisconsin. In 1995, the district attorney in Jefferson County hit Ladish Malting Co., a wholly owned subsidiary of Cargill, Inc., with reckless homicide charges in connection with the death of Vernon Langholff, an employee who had fallen 100 feet from a fire escape landing that broke apart from a grain elevator. State officials alleged that the unsafe condition of the fire escape had been reported to the company's safety committee three years earlier.

But in most such cases, district attorneys are under heavy pressure from big business interests not to bring such prosecutions. In the Hayes case, Patrick's father, Ron Hayes, approached the Florida state's attorney to look at the possibility of criminally prosecuting the company.

"[The state's attorney] told me and my wife and my attorney that he was scared by the company's attorney," Hayes says. "The company's attorney told the state's attorney that they would make this a political issue if the state tried to prosecute. The state's attorney said that he just did not want to get into a political battle. He was not going to try to help us politically with this case."

Even though corporate offenders regularly tilt the legal system to their advantage, some blatant acts of criminality do slip through the cracks and are prosecuted. Forty-six executives were convicted in the "Operation Wind" defense procurement fraud enforcement action in the early 1990s. Thirteen major defense corporations—including Boeing, General Electric, United Technologies and Hughes— were convicted in that operation. In *When the Pentagon Was for Sale*, Andy Pasztor, a *Wall Street Journal* correspondent who covered the Pentagon, tells the inside story of the country's biggest defense scandal. Multi-billion dollar contracts were secretly doled out according to a "shopping list" devoid of any competition, one of the main conspirators recalled to Pasztor. The conspirators assembled their contracts "just the way you would make one out if you went to the supermarket. When you're in control, you can do anything you want, absolutely anything.... And we did."

Meanwhile, Exxon, International Paper, United Technologies, Weyerhaeuser, Pillsbury, Ashland Oil, Texaco, Nabisco and Ralston-Purina have all been convicted of environmental crimes in recent years. Currently, federal grand juries in Manhattan, New Orleans, Washington, D.C., Brooklyn and Alexandria, Virginia are investigating the tobacco industry for a whole range of wrongdoing, from lying to Congress to deceiving shareholders about the known addictive hazards of smoking.

Recidivist corporations steal billions of dollars every year. They are often caught by company whistleblowers and by federal or state officials under the nation's toughest anti-corporate wrongdoing civil law—the federal False Claims Act. The *qui tam* provisions of the False Claims Act permit a private citizen to file suit on behalf of the federal government and collect a portion of the money if the government's action is successful. In 1994, a group of the nation's largest defense contractors worked the halls of Congress in an effort to weaken this law. (The bill later died in a Senate committee.)

In response, a public interest group—the Project on Government Oversight—began to research the records of the companies seeking to weaken this popular anti-fraud law. The project studied the criminal histories of these companies and found that the companies had been engaged in adjudicated fraudulent activities (some criminal)—many of them three or more times.

The study found that General Electric has engaged in fraudulent activities 16 times since 1990. According to the study, a modified "three strikes and you're out" rule would have disqualified an impressive roster of fraud-tainted losers from receiving government contracts, including Boeing (4), Grumman (5), Honeywell (3), Hughes Aircraft (9), Martin Marietta (5), McDonnell Douglas (4), Northrop (4), Raytheon (4), Rockwell (4), Teledyne (5), Texas Instruments (3) and United Technologies (3).

Meanwhile, corporatist politicians, not beholden to any notion of corporate justice, are shameless in their defense of corporate crime. In 1995, a reporter asked Speaker of the House Newt Gingrich about his association with Southwire Co., a major Georgia company convicted of environmental crimes. The reporter pressed Gingrich to explain why he hadn't severed his ties to the family that controls the company and that dumped more than $100,000 into Gingrich's various campaigns and projects.

"You are talking about the largest employer in Carroll County [Gingrich's home base], which has over 3,000 people who work for it," Gingrich said. "I hardly think that having been convicted of a violation turns one into a criminal company." No politician could get away with an answer like this after taking contributions from convicted inner-city drug dealers who put to work thousands of their fellow citizens.

Gingrich was also asked in 1995 about House Republican efforts to limit the criminal liability of doctors and other health care providers who rip off the health care system for an estimated $100 billion a year. "For the moment, I'd rather lock up the murderers, the rapists and the drug dealers," he replied. "Once we start getting some vacant jail space, I'd be glad to look at it." Clearly, Gingrich and the rest of the corporatist Washington crowd fail to grasp a fundamental lesson of effective deterrence: enforce the law against the most powerful members of society first.

Ignore or downplay the crimes of the powerful, and like a fish, respect for legal authority rots from the head down. Why should street criminals respect legal authority when corporatists like Gingrich give the flashing green light to doctors and hospital executives to plunder the health care system?

Gingrich has said we must "re-establish shame as a means of enforcing proper behavior." Who wouldn't agree? But let's start at the top, where the rot takes hold.

"Between 1980 and 1992, the nation's 500 biggest corporations more than doubled their assets from $1.18 trillion to $2.68 trillion. Over the same dozen years, the number of jobs at America's 500 biggest companies fell from 15.9 to 11.5 million."

"In 1992, American corporations spent more on advertising—$134 billion—than they paid in federal corporate income tax. The corporate tax bill for the year: $131 billion."

Too Much: A Quarterly Commentary on Capping Excessive Income and Wealth, Fall 1995, p. 3.

6

Billions for Corporations, Bills for the People

Ralph Nader

Held hostage by and responsible for an economy that is overwhelmingly private and corporate, Presidents tend to cater to the expectations of major corporations, whose demands are transmitted in hundreds of ways from near and far to the White House, the Cabinet, the agencies, the Federal Reserve, Congress and the courts. Presidents find plenty of corporate power to shape the tax system so that liquor and tobacco entertainment expenses are deductible, as are interest payments on loans for mergers, acquisitions and leveraged buyouts. What is lacking is the citizen power essential to prod politicians to enact legislation to replace these wasteful deductions with, for example, deductions for college tuition payments. Presidents find ample business backing for giving away to corporations publicly owned assets such as the minerals on federal lands, the medical innovations of the National Institutes of Health and the public airwaves. Where is the power to reverse these policies?

Corporate power turns Washington into a bazaar of accounts receivable, replete with business subsidies, bailouts, giveaways, grants, inflated contracts and other aids to dependent corporations. Where is the President going to get the political power to represent the small taxpayers and the consumers who end up paying all the bills? In the late 1970s, consumers were denied even a tiny advocacy agency that could fit in a small corner of the Department of Commerce, whose main mission is to promote business profits. There are boundless absurdities in this imbalance of power between the corporate government's domination of the presidency and the weakened tools the people have to control that government. Taxpayers now pay, through the Pentagon budget, for the criminal fines that other agencies impose on defense contractors for toxic contamination. Taxpayers also pay to promote Big Macs and tobacco overseas. Yet they are not even permitted to have a checkoff on their tax return so they can form a taxpayers' advocacy association to protect their tax dollars from legal and illegal looting.

President Clinton wanted to give health insurance coverage to more Americans. How? He had only the power to do what was acceptable to the insurance, hospital, drug and doctor lobbies. These power brokers, not the patients or consumers, have the veto. Notice Clinton's economic policies. They have consisted largely of providing incentives (read corporate welfare payments) to the business community directly or indirectly. His Putting People First agenda flew in the face of reality because the citizenry had no power to make him put people before corporations when the two interests conflicted. Sensitive to who wields daily power, Clinton declined to make a major campaign issue of law and order against widespread corporate crime, fraud and abuse (abetted or permitted under three prior Republican terms).

Unless Presidents deliberately set out to place more democratic tools in the hands of citizens, the White House will simply consolidate the corporate agenda and send the bill to the people. The crimes and debacles of the Savings and Loan industry illustrate the servile quality of Presidents and Congresses, who view themselves primarily as agents of business, serving up a costly feast of corporate socialism for which powerless taxpayers get the bill.

Most politicians in Washington believe that enterprise zones are a major answer to the economic problems of the inner cities. Puerto Rico has been one large enterprise zone for many years and has lavished 'business incentive' after 'business incentive' on corporations. Yet the unemployment rate and poverty in that commonwealth are staggering.

What poor people need is more functioning democracy with which to mobilize communities into action against exploiters and redliners. Absent this, the parameters of the President's urban-policy powers will be largely set by the banking, real estate and insurance lobbies. Nothing illustrates better how presidential power is structurally tilted to favor the powerful corporate interests over the rest of America than the system of ownership without control. The people legally own major national assets: $3 trillion in pension funds, more than $2 trillion in savings deposits, hundreds of billions more in insurance company equity, federal lands (one-third of America), large blocs of shares of companies on the stock exchanges, as well as the airwaves. Although the people own these assets, they do not control any of them. Corporations do. Presidents have ample backup power to preserve this split between ownership and control, but they and Congress have little backup power to make such ownership mean control.

Compared with the hundreds of billions of dollars our government spends perpetuating corporate welfare, building democracy is cheap. It can be done by voluntary checkoffs on tax returns to enable citizens to fund political campaigns instead of the Fortune 500. It can be done by requiring all legal monopolies—electric, gas, telephone and water companies—to include inserts in their bills inviting customers to form their own consumer protection associations. Companies, such as banks, receiving any of the myriad government bailouts and subsidies should be required to do the same thing as a matter of reciprocity. Such mechanisms for communities of people to band together and fund their full-time specialists and advocates cost the taxpayer little or nothing, are universally accessible and may be joined or not.

The three elements of democratic activity—timely information, the technology to communicate with one another, and then mobilization for action and results—could also be served by an Audience Network established by Congressional charter. Voluntary dues-paying members of the Audience Network would support local and national television and radio studios, with producers and reporters programming daily one-hour prime-time shows on the public's airwaves. Moreover, the government itself, through Social Security envelopes, postal service deliveries and many other forms of communication, could provide notices making it easier, state by state, for people to band together in non-profit citizen-action groups.

Washington is a federal forum whose operating slogan has been "Billions for corporations, bills for the people." Without a second-track presidency to build democracy, the first track cannot produce fair solutions because it does not have the necessary civic backbone to overcome the concentrations and abuses of power that breed the many problems that roll so easily off the tongues of politicians at election time.

Societies rot from the top down. They reconstruct from the bottom up. Real democracy is not just good for the economy. It is good for peace and tranquillity, for character and local initiative, for justice and the pursuit of happiness.

Section 2

Redefining the National Interest

Our foreign policy elites have always used the term "national interest" to justify their policies governing our relations with the rest of the world. Yet we seldom ask, "Whose interests are really served by the standard definition of the national interest?"

As the essays in this section make clear, U.S. foreign policy is aimed at helping wealthy elites, to the detriment of most Americans. In "Separating Corporate Interests from the National Interest" Richard Barnet and John Cavanagh cut through the sterile debate between the corporate globalist position and the "America First" position to argue for a new definition of the U.S. national interest. Although James Rinehart's "The Ideology of Competitiveness: Pitting Worker Against Worker" is from a Canadian perspective, his critique of how international competitiveness has become the all-purpose excuse for downsizing rings true for the United States as well. In "Behind the Cloak of Benevolence: World Bank/IMF Policies Hurt Workers at Home and Abroad" Cavanagh, Anderson and Pike provide abundant evidence that the structural adjustment policies pushed on debtor countries have reduced U.S. exports and therefore hurt the U.S. job market. In "Paying to Lose Our Jobs," Patricia Horn explains how the U.S. Agency for International Development uses taxpayers' money to help U.S. corporations move their manufacturing facilities to other countries. "Shattered Promises: The Truth Behind NAFTA's Claims of Job Creation," by Peter Cooper and Lori Wallach, reports the results of their study comparing the promises made by pro-NAFTA corporations when the trade agreement was being

debated and the actual hiring/firing they did after NAFTA became law. Jeremy Rifkin, in his essay "Corporate Technology
and the Threat to Civil Society," argues that new technologies
will be used by corporate leaders to eliminate jobs in the private
sector; the government sector will not be able to fill the job gap;
and the public sector (not-for-profit organizations) will need to
step in and create meaningful jobs.

7

Separating Corporate Interests from the National Interest

Richard Barnet and John Cavanagh

The Cold War defined almost fifty years of history. The collapse of the old order, which came with such suddeness, has left the world in the grip of a continuing process of astounding change and has left the people of the United States in need of leaders with new visions of the national interest based on the new global realities.

Unfortunately, most participants in the current national debate so far have fallen into the trap of a false polarization between an isolationist vision of "America First" and a neo-Cold War vision based on the old-Cold War slogan of "global responsibility." Some of the "America Firsters" employ just a dollop of jingoism, while others flaunt their isolationism, but none show much awareness of the impact of global changes on the lives of the voters whom they are courting. The neoglobalists try to adapt the Cold War vision to the post-Cold War world by proposing modest "downsizing" to a "lean, mobile" military force on guard against all sorts of new, unpredictable dangers. They call upon the United States to take on an even greater "world leadership" role now that the archenemy is gone.

The "America Firsters" argue that we are neglecting our own society by taking on the defense of the world and spending money on other nations. They say it is time to spend more money here, a prescription that even the neoglobalists now share and which has merit. Any plausible threat posed by the Soviet Union has collapsed, and the military hardware, doctrines, and threat assessments developed during the Cold War world are largely obsolete. The consequences of years of neglecting our domestic society are apparent as the recession drags on and the employment, education, housing, and health crises deepen.

Just as national security based on nuclear deterrence was the central idea of the Cold War period, the dominant reality of the new era in world politics is the rapid globalization of much of the world's economic activity. The U.S. economy is now so thoroughly integrated into the global economy that the isolationist option no longer exists. No president of the United States would be able to carry out an isolationist policy without doing great damage to the American people, no matter how overwhelming the mandate to try.

The isolationist option is outmoded for several reasons:

• The great engines of the U.S. economy—banks, industrial corporations and service providers such as worldwide insurance companies, accounting firms, law firms and advertising agencies— are all global actors with loyalties and interests that extend far beyond the shores of this country. No national government can control them, much less force them to serve a nationalistic policy that is not in their interest. At best, our government can influence their behavior in ways that benefit the people and territory of the United States by creating incentives and disincentives.

• Every American worker is part of a global labor pool. Even top executives are now competing with non-Americans for management jobs. (A number of major corporations flying the U.S. flag have CEOs who are foreign nationals.) American factory workers in virtually every industry have been challenged over the past twenty years by increasingly efficient, lower-wage workers across the world. The consequence of the global shift in production is the loss of American jobs and the decline in living standards and expectations for all except the very rich. Protectionism and the economic warfare that such policies inevitably trigger, only accelerate the loss of jobs.

• Environmental problems, from greenhouse gas emissions to acid rain, now threaten everyone. To offer but one prominent example, waste disposal is now a global operation. Rich countries are exporting toxic industrial by-products to poor countries around the world, after decades of burying such materials in their own poorer communities. The global traffic in waste actually complicates the task of governments everywhere. As poorer countries compete with one another to house the industrial waste products of the richer countries and to attract pollution producing industry, the result is not only a lowering of environmental standards but the frustration of environmental policy. Toxic waste does not respect borders. One consequence of environmental deterioration is more refugees and immigrants.

• No national government, including the U.S. government, can control the huge movements of capital that travel across the world via computer at a speed five hundred times the snap of a finger; twenty-four hours a day, every day, more than $500 billion flows through the world's major foreign exchange markets, beyond the reach of any effective regulation. Because money can be borrowed and invested anywhere in the world, national governments can no longer manage their economies effectively by simply adjusting interest rates. In times of inflation or recession, the medicine—raising or lowering the rate—must be administered in such strong doses that dangerous side effects are inescapable.

• The United States is the world's largest debtor nation. Our national government would be unable to meet its payroll unless it received the $100 billion or more a year from the non-American financiers on whom it has come to depend. This dependence necessarily restricts the United States in dealing with its creditors on political matters. The nations that finance the U.S. deficit also happen to be our major commercial rivals. But the isolationist alternatives are either to print more money or slash essential services even further. Neither is a basis for building national strength.

Redefine National Interest

The crisis facing the United States and every other nation-state demands new understandings of what a nation is. National interest is an old-fashioned term. It is most frequently invoked by presidents to describe or to defend whatever they have decided to do. For that reason many people reject the term as vacuous or meaningless. But the term is as good as any to describe a set of principles and understandings that bind a people into a political community. Without at least an intuitive sense of a common commitment to a common destiny, people are unwilling and even unable to sacrifice short-term advantage for the common good.

The rich have abundant opportunities to break their covenant with the nation, and we have seen many examples in recent years: multibillion-dollar scams on Wall Street, the great Savings-and-Loan larceny, and tax avoidance and evasion on a monumental scale. The consequences of these great treasury raids are felt by millions of taxpayers, depositors and investors. The growing economic inequities in the nation, compounded by racial and gender tensions, are becoming more apparent. In the 1980s the average after-tax income of the top one percent of households increased 122 percent, while that of the bottom fifth of households fell 10 percent. Those with money and marketable professional skills can transcend the economic and social problems that beset their fellow citizens. They are mobile. They can invest abroad. They can work abroad. They have the money to buy private education for their children, health care for their families, and to insulate themselves from the crime and squalor all around them. Many enthusiastic flag-wavers with the money and intellectual resources to opt out of a troubled society are disengaging from the nation psychologically, economically, and even physically.

Most Americans cannot follow that course. They are rooted in a place. They are dependent on jobs on American soil. They have little to invest in stock markets that are opening to foreign shareholders all over the world. As the nation becomes more dependent on the global economy, the gulf widens between those who are able to benefit from the age of globalization and those who cannot. The victims of the extraordinary changes in the position and condition of our nation are also withdrawing from the political community that we call the United States of America. In increasing numbers they are turning their backs on politics, giving up on school, trafficking in drugs. Having witnessed the breakup of the Soviet Union, we would do well to realize that nations can collapse in many different ways.

Invest in Environmental Security

The greatest threats to the safety and security of the nation and world are escalating environmental crises and the continued dangers posed by nuclear weapons. It is disturbing that none of our major political leaders has made the environmental crisis the focus of his/her work, for it suggests a complacency about the real dangers that face the nation. The United States, as the leading emitter of greenhouse gases, should take the initiative in setting targets to reduce such emissions. The lurking presence of unknown amounts of toxic wastes buried at U.S. military bases around the world and in hundreds of communities at home poses health and environmental problems that will beset us for decades to come. A massive cleanup effort is long overdue. In addition, investment in improving the environment presents a unique opportunity to stimulate the U.S. economy. Energy efficient and environmentally beneficial technologies could become the basis for a new wave of investment in our industry.

Instead of building up unilateral police forces for missions that are far from clear, the United States should offer to take the lead in facilitating the implementation of the military provisions of the United Nations Charter. As the world's only global military superpower, the United States could play an important role in designing, training, and supplying global and regional police forces under United Nations command. It could take the lead in developing new rules governing the use of such forces and seek to build a consensus on when, where, and by whom police forces will be used. The financing of this effort should be borne substantially by nations that have benefited over the years from the disproportionate investment in military capabilities which the United States has made for the common defense of the non-Communist world.

If these policies were followed, the United States would be safer and stronger than in the Cold War years in two senses. First, the worldwide military environment would be less dangerous than in a world of regional arms races that now threaten to break out into war. Second, substantial funds would be released to repair the basic weaknesses in the nation's industrial base and domestic infrastructure. Before the Soviet Union splintered, a number of former Pentagon officials concluded that our military budget could be cut in half by the year 2000. If the dramatic new opportunities are wisely used, even more substantial savings are possible.

Promote Genuine Democracy

In the Cold War years the United States advanced the idea of democracy in Eastern Europe and the Third World largely as a propaganda weapon in the struggle with the Soviet Union. The conventional wisdom across the political spectrum was that neither Russia nor Third World dictatorships had ever been democracies and that their cultural heritage would keep them from ever becoming democracies. As the Berlin Wall fell, the sheer power of the democratic idea amazed politicians and pundits in the world's richest democracy, which is now looked to more than ever for political inspiration and practical democratic experience. The spread of democracy should be an important goal for the United States. Although free elections do not necessarily guarantee good governments or even friendly ones, the United States is safer and conducts its affairs more honorably when it is dealing with democracies rather than corrupt authoritarian clients.

However, now that the propaganda war has been won, the great danger is that disillusionment borne of economic failure will doom the prospects for democracy in many countries and that chaos will invite the return of tanks and gulags. The United States has a moral obligation as well as a strong national security interest in helping—to the extent it can—to make democracy work in countries in the throes of change. Advice and encouragement are fine, but the United States will make its greatest impact by

pressing for global demilitarization, which will save scarce resources, and by supporting the integration of former one-party
dictatorships into the world economy on reasonable terms that
do not further impoverish them.

The wars, rebellions, and acts of terrorism that we are likely
to see in the post-Cold War order will be the consequences of
frustrations and disappointments over the transition to democracy and the capitalist economy that has nourished democracy in
Western Europe and in the United States. Militarism and genuine
democracy have always been enemies. The United States cannot
advance the cause of democracy either at home or abroad without promoting the vision of a world in which the grip of military
force on politics is broken.

The United States can help raise international capital to finance transitions to democracy. It can take the lead in challenging economic policies that widen the gap between rich and poor
countries and between rich and poor within countries. The United
States has said little in the past about the essential economic component of democracy. The right to free speech and assembly without a realistic hope for a job, decent housing, schooling, and health
care is a recipe for chaos and civil strife, not democracy. Fifty
years ago Franklin Delano Roosevelt articulated the inseparabil-
ity of political and economic rights. Citizens who are no longer
terrorized by their own governments can serve as an added deter-
rent to cheating on disarmament agreements. The international
protection of human rights is now an indispensable component
of an effective security policy. The president of the United States
has the opportunity and the responsibility of leading a global effort to make democracy real.

Reorient Investment Incentives

U.S. corporations have maintained a consistently large share
of world trade only by locating much of their production abroad,
and the result has been deteriorating cities, a massive loss of high-
paying jobs, and mounting economic insecurity for most Americans. Unlike the German and Japanese governments, which have

pursued policies encouraging their own corporations to invest substantially at home in the interest of creating jobs and markets to invigorate their own societies, our government has pursued the opposite course. A series of tax provisions (e.g., tax relief and tax deferral for foreign earnings), a number of trade agreements that allow U.S. firms to pay minimal tariffs on goods imported from their factories in Mexico or the Caribbean, and insurance schemes and loan guarantees (such as the Overseas Private Investment Corporation and the Export-Import Bank) make foreign investment more attractive than investing in the United States.

The United States needs new policies that will reverse the incentive structure and encourage U.S. capital to invest at home. Military industries aside, foreign capital should be welcome under the same conditions. A major new program of reinvestment and reindustrialization should be based on a new covenant between the owners of capital, workers, and the communities where factories and commercial operations are located. The U.S. market is the most valuable asset in American hands. Access to the market, irrespective of the flag that a corporation may fly, should be predicated on corporate behavior that strengthens local economies, improves working conditions, trains workers, and respects the environment. The range of cultural pressures and financial incentives that encourage or permit U.S. corporate managers to pay themselves bloated compensation as their corporations flounder, or to lunge for quick profits instead of long-term investment, must be changed if the U.S. economy is not to become permanently mortgaged to foreign entrepreneurs and creditors. In the interest of economic self-preservation and independence, a new corporate culture should be encouraged by presidential example, even as the irresponsible corporate culture of the 1980s was stimulated by White House rhetoric and behavior. Where appropriate, the guidelines of a new corporate culture should be mandated by law. Just as the European Community is adopting a social charter to protect the newly integrated near-continental economy from the excesses of free trade, so the great continental economy of the United States needs similar protection.

Establish Realistic Trade Policy

A strategy of reinvestment in the United States also requires a shift in trade policy. The United States is increasingly dependent on foreign trade, as indeed are all the other industrial and would-be industrial nations. The Bush administration policy combined the rhetoric of free trade with the increasing use of threats to invoke punitive tariffs and the increasing resort to non-tariff barriers. During the last decade, living standards plummeted in Latin America, Africa, and in large parts of Asia as heavily indebted governments slashed spending and imports. The United States has already felt the consequences: the speedup in illegal drug traffic as governments make desperate efforts to earn foreign exchange and subsistence farmers discover that they can earn a great deal more money growing coca than corn; the flow of refugees from poverty and from the wars spawned by poverty; and the loss of export-related jobs in the United States. (For every $1 billion decline in exports to developing countries that no longer have either the foreign exchange or an employed population large enough to buy American goods, twenty thousand jobs are lost in our economy, according to the U.S. Department of Commerce.) Clearly, it is impossible to insulate the United States from the poverty that afflicts two-thirds of the world's people.

Free trade in the absence of enforceable standards guaranteeing a decent minimum level of pay and dignified working conditions will impoverish working people in the United States. When U.S.-based and foreign firms can choose between paying $7 an hour here or $4 a day in Mexico, the consequences are clear. Either factories will move to Mexico or our workers will find themselves under increasing pressure to accept wages closer to Mexican levels. The effects of the lowering of global working conditions have already been felt in the United States. Present trends whereby global standards are heading inexorably downward, increasingly driven toward the lowest common denominator, can only be reversed through enforceable international standards with respect to health, safety, worker rights and compensation, social welfare, and the environment.

Just as labor and social welfare laws accompanied the emergence of a more unified domestic U.S. economy a half century ago, the new global marketplace needs global rules. The best instruments for introducing global standards are trade agreements. The United States should take the lead in calling for the revision of the General Agreement on Tariffs and Trade, the global trade compact concluded at the end of World War II, to include legally binding and enforceable provisions for protecting worker rights, mandating minimum levels of social investment, and setting out environmental standards. The same mechanisms should be an integral and indispensable part of any regional trade agreement such as the North American Free Trade Agreement.

Eliminate Inequalities and Reduce Debt

The long-term economic problem facing the United States and the global economy is that too many industrial countries are trying to sell the same basket of goods to that shrinking proportion of the global population with enough money to buy them. While the world population is growing at a dramatic rate, the number of people who can afford globally produced goods is not growing at all—with the exception of consumers of very few cheap products like cigarettes and soft drinks. The structural problems facing the world economy require policies that address the growing inequalities that limit purchasing power in so much of the world.

After the spectacular postwar spurt of the 1950s and 1960s, growth in world trade slackened off. While a few countries in Asia have shown phenomenal growth—thanks in part to the willingness of the United States to accept a flood of imports largely financed by consumer debt—world trade as a whole has been stalled.

The economic policies of recent decades have widened the gap between rich and poor and slowed the growth of the middle class on whom global mass markets depend. Because of the debt burden in the developing world, poor countries now pay about $50 billion more to banks and other creditors in rich countries than they receive in new loans. After World War II, the world economy was stimulated by the United States with farsighted aid programs for war-ravaged Europe and Japan. Now there is no money for a new global Marshall Plan for poor countries that some have advocated over the years. But it is possible to stop the *reverse* Marshall Plan from underdeveloped countries to their rich creditors by adopting realistic and far-reaching debt reduction programs instead of the policies now imposed by the International Monetary Fund (IMF). If the impact of austerity is the further impoverishment of large areas of the world, the costs are eventually borne by working people in the rich countries.

It is not easy to ascertain with precision the moral and psychological consequences of living in a world in which starvation, epidemics, environmental disasters, and endless bloody strife are nightly television fare. Over a century ago, Abraham Lincoln summoned the nation to listen to the better angels of our nature; surely these include generosity and a welcoming spirit. Americans today cannot turn their backs on the suffering of the world without losing some of the spirit that built the nation, indeed without becoming a lesser people. The environmental consequences of extreme economic pressures in poor countries, such as the indiscriminate rain forest destruction which has accelerated the emission of greenhouse gases, are evident. So are the refugee flows and the public health consequences of the AIDS epidemic, neither of which respect borders. In the post-Cold War world the best defense is not offense but an intelligent set of policies to address the causes of global violence.

Nike's Exploited Workers

Medea Benjamin

During the 1970s, most Nike shoes were made in South Korea and Taiwan. When workers there gained new freedom to organize and wages began to rise, Nike looked for "greener pastures." It found Indonesia, where it started producing shoes in 1986.

Indonesia has a repressive regime that outlaws independent unions and sets the minimum wage at rock bottom—below the subsistence level for one person. In 1996, the entry-level wage was a miserable $2.20 a day. A livable wage in Indonesia is about $4.25 a day.

Compare this with the pay of Nike's executives and celebrity promoters. CEO Philip Knight is worth over $5 billion. Michael Jordan gets $20 million a year to promote Nike sneakers. Jordan's compensation alone would be enough to raise Nike's Indonesian workforce out of poverty.

Despite Indonesia's repressive government, workers in the shoe industry have been rebelling against low pay, forced overtime, abusive treatment by factory managers and lack of health and safety standards. When the foreign press publicized these abuses, Nike denied responsibility. It insisted that Nike did not own the factories, it contracted the work to independent sub-contractors.

Yet with mounting criticism, Nike relented and in 1992 came up with a Code of Conduct that set standards for its contractors. But abuses continued; workers demanding better conditions were dismissed and independent organizing was still prohibited.

Labor, religious and consumer groups have increased their anti-Nike organizing. They demand that Nike agree to independent monitoring of their factories by local human rights groups, that the company settle claims by workers who were unfairly dismissed, that independent organizing be allowed in Nike factories, and that wages and working conditions be improved.

[For information on the Nike campaign call Global Exchange at (415) 255-7296.]

8

The Ideology of Competitiveness: Pitting Worker Against Worker

James Rinehart

The necessity of competitiveness has been hammered home by governments, corporations, and the media to the point that it is taken for granted, a fact of life that is so obvious that we unthinkingly acquiesce to its dictates. Competitiveness has been elevated to the status of a natural law, like the law of gravity, a force that is useless to question or resist. In part, the seductiveness of the term arises from its roots in the material process of economic competition.

Monopolies and oligopolies notwithstanding, some degree of competition between business firms for markets and profits is an inherent element of capitalism that can be observed and measured. In contrast, competitiveness, or the ideology of competition, is used to justify the decisions and actions of firms, especially when the outcomes adversely affect some people, groups, and classes. Historically, the concept of competitiveness has been used to justify business opposition to: unions, reduced hours of work, wage increases, paid vacations, health and safety regulations and anti-pollution laws.

In recent years, competitiveness has been invoked with increasing frequency and has taken on new usages. We are led to believe that enhancing corporate or national competitiveness is in everyone's interest, a win-win game with no losers, at least in the long run. More and more, competitiveness is used as a form of blackmail.

Corporations and financial capitalists threaten to withhold or relocate investment if workers refuse to grant concessions or if government regulations and spending on social programs are too great. The word competitiveness now is used to justify actions that increase profitability even when firms are not facing declining markets and profits. Finally, the use of competitiveness is no longer restricted to the economic sphere. Increasingly, governments invoke the term to legitimize relaxing regulations on corporations and removing barriers to corporate profitability (most notably enshrined in free trade agreements), such as spending on unemployment compensation, health, education and welfare.

We are told repeatedly that the drive for competitiveness is in the best interests of both employees and employers. Workers are told they must cooperate and become partners with the managers of their companies, they must pull together, do more with less, get lean and mean, to beat out the competition. Only then will their jobs be secure. In this scenario, workers in one country are pitted against those in all others. Canadian workers in one auto, chemical, or insurance company are pitted against Canadian workers in other auto, chemical, and insurance companies in a race for competitive advantage and job security.

Not long ago a rally attended by about 1,000 employees was held in a large tent outside the Ford plant in Oakville, Ontario. The company passed out refreshments and baseball caps with company logos, and managers spoke about the troubled future of the plant. The plant manager said Ford had 6.5 million excess vehicles, that the plant's Topaz and Tempo models didn't measure up to a competitor's model, the Toyota Camry, and that the Oakville plant had higher absenteeism, lower productivity, and more grievances than a sister plant in Kansas City that also produced the Topaz and Tempo. The message being conveyed—that Oakville could be shut down—was a frightening one, a possibility strengthened by these Ford workers having seen plant after plant in southern Ontario shut down, including the Mack Truck plant across the street. A video was shown of a small-town Pennsylvania football team that produced perennial champions. The message was clear: if you work hard enough, you too can play on a winning team. The speeches had the tone of sermons at a religious revival meeting (also traditionally held in large tents), only in Oakville salvation comes not from faith and good deeds but from working harder, doing more with less, and cooperating with management. The plant manager then made a dramatic announcement. A top manager from Kansas City had just joined the Oakville team. Everyone cheered. The former Kansas City manager appeared on stage and gave a pep talk, assuring the workers that Oakville was a winner. "Watch out, Kansas City," he yelled. "Watch out, Toyota Camry, here comes Oakville." At this point everyone jumped up, threw their hats in the air, clapped, and cheered, as loud rock and roll music with a heavy bass beat filled the tent.

Undoubtedly, Ford workers in Kansas City attended the same kind of pep rally, the only difference being the enemy— Ford Oakville. This same kind of scenario is played out less obviously, but no less destructively, for workers at the community, provincial, state, national and international levels.

While workers compete against each other in a concessions race to the bottom, corporations have found ways of avoiding or cushioning dog-eat-dog competition. Ford owns 25 percent of Mazda and has joint ventures with Volkswagen; General Motors has joint ventures with Toyota, Suzuki, and Fiat; Chrysler allied with Mitsubishi. If you buy a Pontiac Le Mans from GM for, say, $10,000, $3,000 goes to South Korea for assembly labor; $1,750 to Japan for engines, transaxles, and electronics; $750 to Germany for styling and design; $400 to Taiwan, Singapore, and Japan for small components; $250 to England for advertising and marketing services; and $50 to Ireland and Barbados for data processing.

While workers around the world compete, it is not usually Indonesian, Philippine, or Mexican firms that compete with U.S. or Canadian firms. Instead it is often subsidiaries of General Electric, Northern Telecom, or General Motors, for example, located in one of these countries "competing" against their own plants in

North America. Those who are most caught up in the struggle for existence are workers, not major corporations, three hundred of which now own about one-quarter of the productive assets of the world. Of the richest one hundred economies of the world, forty-seven are corporations, not nations.

What these examples suggest is that the ideology of competitiveness greatly exaggerates real levels of interfirm competition among the largest players.

In Adam Smith's eighteenth century vision of economics, competition was undertaken via price cuts of goods and services. But one wonders about the advantage to consumers of competitiveness when a firm like Nike can produce sports shoes in Indonesia for a total cost of $5.60 and sell those same shoes in Europe and North America for anywhere from $70 to $135. Competitiveness now means *not* cheap prices but which workers, which taxpayers, which provinces, and which countries can give the most to the corporation in exchange for new investment or to insure that work does not move elsewhere.

On July 8, 1992, *Toronto Globe and Mail* business editor Terrance Corcoran praised South Carolina because it was able to lure BMW to build a new auto plant there. The bait? Cheap labor, the lowest corporate taxes in the United States, absence of unions ("right-to-work" state), 40 million tax dollars to upgrade a local airport, a massive infusion of tax dollars for training grants, and a state run and financed recruitment and training facility at taxpayers expense. Corcoran concluded his article with this message: "Wake up!" Even if BMW officials had looked at Ontario or other parts of Canada, what would they have found? (Needless to say, Corcoran's vision of an optimally competitive Canada hardly coincides with the kind of country that most of us would want to live in.)

Corporations threaten to withhold or relocate investment (and jobs) to whipsaw workers. They do the same with governments. Restrictions placed on corporations, removal of their tax breaks, increased corporate taxation, laws facilitating unionization, anti-scab laws, and so on, are defined as barriers to competitiveness.

For example, in February 1995 the Ontario government announced it might consider limiting overtime in order to create jobs by spreading around the work. The corporate response was immediate. GM of Canada's answer was typical: "Ultimately, it is going to have a negative effect on our bottom line. We would be working at a competitive disadvantage to our southern neighbors who have no restrictions on the amount of overtime they can work."

In the public sector, deficits and debt take on the same function as competitiveness in the private sector. Efforts to fight the debt also are justified by the argument that such action will enhance Canada's competitiveness. We have witnessed more and more cutbacks in public sector jobs and services. In the first five months of 1995, 74,000 public administration jobs (8.2 percent of the total) at the federal, provincial, and municipal levels were chopped; 20,000 more federal jobs were scheduled to disappear in 1995, and by 1998 the total will reach 45,000. To get a sense of the devastation, we must add wage freezes, back-to-work legislation, and the piece by piece dismantling of social programs. All this is undertaken to create, as they say, a level playing field that will enhance Canada's competitiveness.

Corporations have always responded to declining markets and sales by cutting back their workforces and putting pressure on employees to work harder for less. But what is new is that these measures are now being taken by highly secure and profitable companies that justify their actions by the need to remain competitive in the future. Corporate profitability and competitiveness do not guarantee job security. The *Wall Street Journal* reported that during the 1990-1991 recession, laid-off workers were told of a "tough new world" in which global competition and technological change required constant leanness, but most employees assumed that the layoffs would stop when good times returned. They were wrong. While corporate profits soared to record levels in 1994, the number of job cuts approached those seen at the height of the recession. Both in 1991 (a bad year for profits) and 1994 (a good year for profits), U.S. corporations cut between 500,000 and 600,000 jobs. In April 1995, Mobil Corporation announced plans to cut 4,700 jobs, even though its first-quarter earnings had reached record levels. While workers lost their jobs, Mobil stockholders laughed all the way to the bank. Just after the cutback announcement, Mobil stock rose to a one-year high. Proctor and Gamble did the same, despite soaring profits. After slashing 13,000 jobs, the P&G chairman said, "We must slim down to stay competitive." He added, "The public has come to think of corporate restructuring as a sign of trouble, but this is definitely not our situation."

Government and business spokespersons maintain that to be competitive Canada should adopt a high-tech development strategy. Since we can't compete with Third World countries on wages, we should encourage industrial growth in sectors where labor costs are a small fraction of total production costs. High-tech industry, we are told, will help restore competitiveness, relieve unemployment, and provide complex, well-paying jobs. The evidence does not bear out this optimism. First, many jobs connected with high-tech (e.g., in the electronics industry) employ a large number of relatively unskilled (mainly women) workers doing light assembly jobs: jobs that are vulnerable to threats to move production off-shore. Second, high-tech firms are slashing their workforces as rapidly as traditional companies. Firms like AT&T, IBM, Xerox, GTE, Ameritech, Apple and other giants in the field are in the process of reducing their workforces by 9 to 22 percent.

Between 1988 and 1992, employment declined by nearly 20 percent in these high-tech industries in Canada: machinery, communications equipment, electrical machinery, aircraft, and office, store and business equipment. Only in pharmaceuticals did high-tech employment grow, and ironically much of this growth was due to job guarantees given in exchange for the Canadian government's extension of patent rights on drugs (i.e., protection against competition from the generic drug producers).

Northern Telecom is a good example of our dubious high-tech future. Nortel became a world leader not through fierce competition but through a regulated telecommunications industry that gave its parent, BellCanada, a market monopoly, which was a major consideration in the company's commitment to R&D and expansion in Canada. Nortel now operates in forty countries and is rapidly expanding its foreign (mostly non-union) operations. In 1994 Nortel had profits of $404 million and expected profits of $550 million in 1995, yet it is making massive cutbacks in its Canadian operations. Over the past five years, the company has closed plants in St. John, New Brunswick, and London, Ontario, has put its Kingston, Ontario plant up for sale, and has planned to chop 1,000 full-time jobs from its facility in Bramalea, Ontario.

The continuous implementation of new technology, the small size of the high-tech sector to begin with, and the tendency to disperse production around the world limit high-tech employment opportunities. As micro-technology finds more and more realms of application, the most rapidly growing jobs will require little training and minimal skill. Projections to the year 2005 from the U.S. Bureau of Labor Statistics indicate that of the 30 fastest growing professions (in terms of number of job openings) only systems analysis, computer engineering and science are directly linked to micro or high technology. The greatest demand will be for retail sales clerks, cashiers, truck drivers, health care workers, waiters, waitresses, cooks, janitors and guards.

These projections also reveal that Canada's high unemployment rate and so-called lack of competitiveness cannot be attributed to an under-educated, under-trained labor force. Victim blaming is rife in business circles, but we hear much less about the management- or investor-induced economic problems related to corporate takeovers and mergers, leveraged buy-outs, financial speculation, risky investment in derivatives and other forms of often profitable but nonproductive investment.

As the good jobs disappear, new ones tend to be part-time, temporary or contracted out. In April 1995, Statistics Canada reported a loss of 17,000 full-time jobs, but part-time employment increased by 17,000. This is simply the latest phase of a longer term trend: 46 percent of the jobs created between 1975 and 1993 were part-time, and by 1993 almost one-quarter (23 percent) of all jobs in Canada offered less than thirty hours of work a week.

Competitiveness means not only fewer full-time jobs but also that all jobs are subject to heavy work loads, constant speedup, and overtime. Recently we were warned by Massachusetts Institute of Technology researchers that in this rough and tumble world only manufacturers who adopt the production and management techniques of the Japanese—a system known as lean production—will survive. Lean production is heralded by the MIT group as beneficial to workers and companies. Workers allegedly are well trained, multi-skilled, perform challenging jobs, and are encouraged to use their knowledge to improve operations.

Research at CAMI, a unionized General Motors-Suzuki auto assembly plant just outside London, Ontario, that uses lean production methods, has revealed a very different picture. At CAMI, as at other lean production plants, most jobs are easily learned, highly standardized, and repetitive, with time cycles ranging from 1.5 to 3 minutes. Workers receive very little training. Much of it is ideological indoctrination, with an emphasis on cultivating the view that all employees, from the president to the production worker, constitute one big team pulling together to beat out the competition. The plant is chronically understaffed, work loads are heavy, rates of repetitive strain injuries are high, and labor-management relations are contentious—this is just skimming the surface. We concluded from our research that lean production— "the wave of the future"—is a system that strives to operate with minimal labor inputs. It is a system whose objective is to take time out of labor and labor out of production. It is a system that aspires to the elimination of all production buffers save one— workers who will toil harder and longer whenever required. In the Fall of 1992, CAMI workers, members of the Canadian Auto Workers union, struck the plant for five weeks. This first-ever strike of a North American transplant or joint venture shattered illusions about harmonious labor-management relations under Japanese production management.

What are we to conclude from these trends? Corporations and the media bombard us with the message that enhanced competitiveness is the answer to our economic woes, including unemployment. What's missing from these pronouncements is any discussion of exactly how (and when) most of us will benefit from competitiveness. Few would question the competitive capacity of Northern Telecom or Nike, but their competitiveness has not been associated with growing prosperity and employment opportunities, either in their home countries or in the Third World where many of their operations are located. As the connection between corporate success and national prosperity becomes ever more tenuous, the urgent question is competitiveness for what and for whom? Buying into competitiveness means accepting the right of big business interests to unilaterally determine our future. Competitiveness involves a race to the bottom. There is no end, no stopping point, no time when the corporation will say, "All right, we have reached our targets; now we can increase wages, stop chopping and overloading jobs." This means continuous rounds of cutbacks and concessions, as there will always be workers somewhere in the world who are desperate enough to work more cheaply. Former Canadian Member of Parliament Donald Blenkarn candidly defined competitiveness: "The Canadian worker can either work harder for less money, or not work at all. That's what competitiveness means."

Corporations and governments ask workers to tighten their belts but rarely mention that executive compensation continues to rise, while the incomes of working people stagnate. Those who ask for sacrifices, obviously enough, never impose the same on themselves. Bertolt Brecht made the point well: "Those who take the meat from the table teach contentment. Those for whom taxes are destined demand sacrifice. Those who eat their fill speak to the hungry of wonderful times to come. Those who lead the country into the abyss call ruling too difficult for ordinary people."

Instead of buying into the ideology of competitiveness, we should be searching for ways to combat the corporate agenda, to extend democratic decision-making into all spheres of life, especially the economic sphere, and to develop peoples' intellectual and cooperative capacities. We need a peoples' agenda not a big business agenda. It has to be a process that starts at home but develops ever broader, more inclusive forms of solidarity and action. Easy to say, tough to do, but it's the only alternative.

"Americans want something more substantial than an invisible hand: 95% of 1,004 adults surveyed in a *Business Week*/Harris Poll rejected the view that corporations' only role is to make money."

Business Week, March 11, 1996, p. 60.

Behind the Cloak of Benevolence: World Bank and IMF Policies Hurt Workers At Home and Abroad

John Cavanagh, Sarah Anderson and Jill Pike

Through a detailed analysis of the impact of IMF (International Monetary Fund) and World Bank lending over the past decade, we have reached the following conclusions.

1. The United States has lost over $1 billion in exports per year because of the recessionary impact of IMF and World Bank policy-based lending. This translates into about 20,500 U.S. jobs lost each year.

2. Of the 54 countries that received major World Bank and IMF policy-based loans between 1980 and 1989, 33 slowed down their imports of U.S. goods, which reduced U.S. jobs.

3. The conditions placed on these loans also hurt workers in the developing world through wage freezes, higher prices on imported goods due to devaluations, higher prices on basic necessities as price supports were cut, and other policy changes.

4. These findings contradict a May 1994 U.S. Treasury Department study that alleges (with no substantiation) that around 100,000 U.S. jobs are created each year because of multilateral development bank policy-based lending.

Background

Supporters of the World Bank and the International Monetary Fund (IMF) are making extravagant claims about the benefits of their operations on the world's environment, consumers and workers. In May 1994, the U.S. Treasury Department released a major study that claimed that the policies of these two institutions stimulate enough growth in the developing world to create an extra $5 billion in U.S. exports each year, adding some 100,000 jobs to the U.S. economy.[1] Drawing from the study, former Treasury Secretary Lloyd Bentsen and Under Secretary Lawrence Summers repeated these job claims in Congressional testimony.[2]

Many in the development and labor communities found these to be extraordinary claims since World Bank and IMF policy prescriptions typically involve a series of measures that dampen developing country imports. The authors of this study made inquiries to the Treasury Department and spoke twice with one of the study's authors; both times he refused to divulge his methodology or tell us how he arrived at his conclusions.

The IMF, the World Bank and U.S. Jobs

Our own detailed study of World Bank and IMF lending concludes that the U.S. Treasury Department claims are patently false. Not only does Bank and Fund policy-based lending not increase U.S. jobs; it actually destroys over 20,000 a year.

Our findings are based on a careful study of all countries that received high conditionality, policy-based loans from the World Bank and IMF over the 1980s. These include the World Bank's structural adjustment loans (SALs), which were initiated in 1980, and the IMF's extended fund facilities (EFF) and structural adjustment facility (SAF).

We studied 54 recipient countries of these loans and in each case we looked at how U.S. exports responded to the policy-based loan (for countries that received more than one loan, we looked at the first loan). In each of the countries we calculated the growth rate of U.S. exports over the three years preceding the loan, and compared it to the rate in the three years after the loan year. The U.S. Commerce Department estimates that a billion dollars of U.S. exports translates into roughly 20,000 U.S. jobs; hence one can estimate how the growth or decline of U.S.

exports to a country affects U.S. jobs. We should add here that University of Illinois professor Dave Ranney and others have shown the fallacy of the Commerce Department's automatic assumption that firms translate increased exports into more jobs. However, firms almost always react to falling exports by cutting jobs.

These are our findings:

• Overall, U.S. exports to the 54 countries were growing at a rate of 8.1 percent in the years prior to the loan. In the years following the loan, the growth rate fell to 6.2 percent. Had the earlier growth rate persisted into the post-loan period, there would have been an extra $1.025 billion worth of U.S. exports each year. Hence, the policy-based lending contributed to a loss of 20,500 U.S. jobs each year.

• Growth in U.S. exports declined in 33 of the 54 countries after the loan. Hence, U.S. jobs were lost in over three-fifths of the cases.

Unlike the authors of the Treasury Department study, we would be the first to acknowledge that many factors influence U.S. exports to a specific country. However, inasmuch as World Bank and IMF policy-based loans and the conditions attached to them have a major impact on developing countries' macro-economic policy framework, these loans directly affect the climate for trade.

The reasons why World Bank and IMF policy-based lending have a negative impact on U.S. exports and hence, U.S. jobs, are quite straightforward.

• Many of the loans prescribe currency devaluations, which have the effect of making imports of U.S. and other products more expensive;

• The loans prescribe cuts in government spending which eliminate government jobs and hence cut purchasing power;

• Many of the loans push for the elimination of government subsidies on the prices of locally-produced basic necessities, which decreases the income people have to spend on U.S. goods;

• In more recent years, many of the loans prescribe a

privatization agenda, which in most developing countries has cost jobs, which again cuts the purchasing power of people to buy U.S. goods.

This chapter focuses on how World Bank and IMF structural adjustment programs hurt U.S. jobs by slowing the growth of U.S. exports. It must be noted, however, that these programs also destroy U.S. jobs by promoting policies that encourage U.S. firms to shift production offshore. Many of the loans are conditioned on the creation of export processing zones, which provide cheap labor and a liberal regulatory environment to attract foreign investors. Low-wage assembly plants in the zones now employ more than 735,000 workers in the Caribbean Basin and Mexico alone. Thousands of U.S. workers have lost their jobs, while hundreds of thousands more experience increased job insecurity as a result of these programs. A National Labor Committee study of export processing zones in El Salvador, Guatemala, and Honduras found that 30 U.S. apparel manufacturers had plants in these countries and another 68 were sourcing from them. Between 1990 and 1992, those same companies had been involved in 58 plant closings and 11 mass layoffs in the United States.[3]

There are two aspects of multilateral development bank loans which do encourage imports from the United States. The first is that the Bank and Fund press countries to liberalize imports through lower tariff and non-tariff barriers to trade. The second area, as advertised heavily in the Treasury Department study, is that in project loans the recipient country often uses part of the proceeds to purchase goods or services from U.S. firms. However, the impact of these policies is seldom enough to offset the anti-import effects of the other policies.

IMF/World Bank and Jobs in the Developing World

Just as the U.S. Treasury Department claims that adjustment policies are good for U.S. jobs, so have the Bank and Fund insisted for years that their policies are good for workers in the developing world. There is now ample evidence that this is false. World Bank structural adjustment loans and the various IMF facilities instead translate into an increase in economic hardship for millions of workers and farmers and their families throughout the developing world through at least six mechanisms, listed below. And, since this growing economic hardship increases instability and dampens consumer demand in poor countries, it has a negative boomerang effect on the United States.

1. *Massive Public Sector Layoffs*

Bank and Fund policies in poor countries can be summed up in four words: "Spend less, export more." As governments attempt to cut expenditures, civil service downsizing is often one of the first targets. Morocco's cuts in public service employees in the wake of its 1981 Extended Fund Facility, for example, contributed to a 60 percent rise in unemployment in that country between 1982 and 1984.[4] A similar process occurred in the Ivory Coast where public sector layoffs followed a 1981 EFF. Had it not been for the absorptive capacity of the informal sector, where incomes are low and uncertain, the official unemployment rate by the early 1990s would have stood at 42 percent rather than 29 percent.[5] African trade unionists have pointed out that the multilateral banks would have done better to pressure governments to reduce bloated military budgets and cut widespread embezzlement of money by government and political party officials.[6]

2. *Spending Cuts in Basic Social Services*

In addition to public sector layoffs, governments have been pressed by adjustment loans to cut basic social services. As education, health care, and other social program budgets are cut, not only are jobs lost directly but the future health and productivity of the workforce are undermined. Ghana received more structural adjustment loans than any other African country between 1983 and 1990. Yet throughout the 1980s, education spending stalled at half of its 1975 levels, and overall enrollment rates declined from 1983 to 1987.[7] During the same period, health spending in Costa Rica fell; the country began its structural adjustment in 1981, and by 1985, the Ministry of Health reported

significant increases in the occurrence of intestinal parasitic diseases, rheumatic fever and alcoholism. Cuts in the Costa Rican
health budget have greatly weakened the capacity of what was
one of Latin America's best public health systems.

3. *Crippling Wage Freezes and Labor Suppression*
The Bank and Fund also press countries to slow or stop the
rise in wages, both to attract foreign investment and to repress
consumer demand. In some countries, the lending programs have
also undercut workers by promoting the suppression of labor
rights. Most recently, a World Bank loan for Nicaragua voted in
July 1994 required the Nicaraguan government to adopt measures that undermine collective contracts, weaken public sector
unions, and remove non-monetary benefits from labor agreements.[8] In country after country undergoing adjustment, workers' purchasing power drops as wages stagnate while prices rise.

4. *Devaluation of Local Currencies*
One of the prominent reasons why workers face rising prices
in adjusting countries is the common policy prescription that
countries should devalue their currency. Devaluations have the
effect of making a country's exports cheaper and its imports more
expensive.

5. *Promotion of Export-Oriented Production*
The Bank and Fund pursue a series of policies in addition to
devaluation to encourage countries to shift more land from basic
food crops to export-oriented production of shrimp, broccoli, cut
flowers, coffee, and dozens of other products. In addition to has-
tening ecological decline (shrimp farms can ruin the water table;
the cash crops often rely on more chemical inputs), this shift has
often been accompanied by rising malnutrition as basic food
prices rise and millions of peasants and indigenous people are
displaced from their land. The World Bank has also been a big
promoter of "free trade zones" where young women often work
in exploitative conditions to produce light manufactured goods

for export to Wal-Mart, Sears, K-mart and other outlets. While a small elite gains from these new export ventures, the rising inequalities between the winners and the workers creates new tensions and instabilities.

6. *Abolition of Price Controls on Basic Foodstuffs*

A favorite target of IMF and World Bank policies is the low prices on basic necessities that governments often subsidize in urban areas. The elimination of these subsidies can be devastating and in several countries, has led to riots and bloodshed. Mozambique received its first IMF Structural Adjustment Facility in 1987. By 1988, prices of basic commodities had shot up exponentially. In the space of one month (March to April), the price of rice rose from 20 cents a kilogram to $1.35; sugar from 25 cents to $1.32; and maize from 14 to 56 cents.[9] A trained secondary school teacher with nine years of basic education and three years of professional training reported spending the dollar equivalent of almost $100 of his monthly $120 salary on basic necessities. Two wage hikes during 1988, of 50 and 15 percent, could not come close to compensating for the 300-500 percent price increases in basic commodities.[10]

In sum, in their zeal to correct macro-economic imbalances and speed the generation of foreign exchange to repay creditors in the rich countries, the IMF and World Bank have visited enormous suffering on the workers of the poorer two-thirds of the world.

Conclusion

Other analysts of the U.S.-based "50 Years is Enough" campaign have offered detailed reports of how the World Bank and IMF have hurt the environment and communities across the developing world. The campaign has put forward a careful argument for reducing, reorganizing and democratizing these institutions. The adverse impact of IMF and World Bank lending on jobs at home and abroad offers one more reason why a major restructuring of these institutions is long overdue.

It is also quite disturbing that the U.S. Treasury Department has thus far been able to get away with using statistical conclusions which are not footnoted and refusing to release the methodology or data on which their conclusions are based. It is difficult to conclude anything other than that the Treasury Department is manipulating figures for political purposes. Treasury officials offer glowing testimony of the multilateral development banks in order to argue for new capital increases from Congress. What better pitch than to claim that they create U.S. jobs. Yet both intuition and a careful study of the figures indicate that the policy-based lending of these agencies *hurts* U.S. jobs in most cases. The American people deserve better from their government.

"I worked in the office as a production planner, managing the inventory supply system. I gave the company my best years, my most productive years and now it's like I've just come out of school looking for my first job. I've missed the boat, I realize that. These kind of jobs just aren't there any more, not for people my age. Companies like Bendix don't really have any feelings for their employees; in the end the buck is the bottom line. If they had their way, management would have robots doing everything in the plant, but they forget that robots don't buy anything."

Bob, 49 years old, a 19-year employee of Bendix Corp., quoted in *New Internationalist*, August 1993.

10

Paying to Lose Our Jobs: The U.S. Job Export Strategy

Patricia Horn

Over the last decade, the federal government has been in the business of exporting U.S. workers' jobs. Over 300 workers in Decaturville, Tennessee, found that out when they lost their jobs after Perry Manufacturing moved its apparel work to El Salvador. So did 72 workers in Newberry, South Carolina; 237 in Wewoka, Oklahoma; 114 in Millersburg, Pennsylvania; and countless other workers in communities across the United States.

The rest of the country found out about the U.S. Agency for International Development-funded program when the National Labor Committee (NLC) released "Paying to Lose Our Jobs" in September 1992. The report revealed how the federal government, through the Agency for International Development (AID), has persuaded factories throughout the United States, particularly in the Southeast, to relocate to low-wage Caribbean and Central American countries. AID promoted the region's "natural comparative advantages"—low wages, no unions and U.S. taxpayer assistance.

"Paying to Lose Our Jobs" also details how, between 1980 and 1993, the Reagan and Bush administrations funneled more than a billion dollars to investment and trade promotion projects in Central America and the Caribbean through AID. At least half of that money went directly to promote company flight to export-processing, or "free trade" zones in those countries.

Thousands of U.S. workers have lost their jobs as a result,

especially in the apparel and electronics industries. In its partial survey of job loss in the apparel industry, the NLC found that—just since 1990—U.S. companies with plants in El Salvador, Guatemala and Honduras have closed 58 plants and conducted 11 mass layoffs that left over 12,000 U.S. workers jobless. Such job loss has helped drive down the wages of remaining apparel workers.

The findings of "Paying to Lose Our Jobs" ripped through the federal government. During its investigation, the staff of NLC worked with the CBS-TV news program "60 Minutes" to film a segment that aired to 50 million viewers three days before the NLC released its report and only a week before Congress began debating the U.S. foreign assistance budget. ABC-TV's "Nightline" picked up the story and ran with it for the following two nights. Donahue devoted a show to the report. And the Clinton/Gore presidential campaign, discovering a wildly popular issue, preached AID's evils at every campaign stop.

Within 10 days of the report's release, both houses of Congress had passed bills prohibiting AID from spending money on export processing zones, from funding projects that violate internationally recognized workers' rights, and from inducing companies to move offshore. Within two months the acting director of AID, Ronald Roskens, resigned. The Congressional Research Office investigated the program. The Government Accounting Office (GAO) set up its own year-long investigation, devoting five staff people to uncover any other federal agency involvement.

"[The response to this report] proves that people care about plant closings," says Charles Kernaghan, the NLC's executive director. "They will care even more when you remove the veil that hides government policy and the effect of worker's rights violations offshore on jobs in this country."

The legislation that outlawed the AID program has slowed migration of apparel factories south, but will not stop the underlying low-wage, job-export strategy the United States is pushing around the globe. The NLC believes that it has only begun to uncover the breadth of the AID program, and, perhaps, of programs of other government agencies.

This Is Development?

"Trade Not Aid" is the nickname of AID's Private Enterprise Initiative, a development plan that has failed everyone except the relocated manufacturers. The professed goal of the program, initiated as the foreign aid part of the Caribbean Basin Initiative (CBI) during President Ronald Reagan's first term, was to create new private investment in Central America and the Caribbean in special export-processing zones. While most foreign assistance previously went to governments, AID sent its money directly to private companies to "foster growth of productive, self-sustaining income and job producing private enterprise in developing countries," as the agency put it.

To those concerned about Third World development, the AID program may not sound like such a bad deal. The jobs lost in the United States create new jobs in Central America and the Caribbean. Except the new jobs in export processing zones are no bargain for workers or local economies. These zones, also known as *maquiladoras*, free-trade, or tax-free zones, typically set themselves up in industrial parks with clear boundaries. They are considered exempt from most of their host country's customs, tax and trade laws.

What makes zones hard on workers is this isolation. Frequently, zone managers barricade the area behind guards and chain link fences topped with barbed wire. The companies pay their workers 40 to 50 cents an hour, a below poverty-level wage even by these countries' standards. And any hint of organizing to fight for better working conditions routinely results in a worker being fired and her name added to the country's "blacklist," ensuring she will never work in a zone again.

According to many development experts, the zone program, along with the CBI, has harmed developing countries. A United Nation's report examined this development strategy. It found that zones stymie potential development because the industries that typically locate in them segregate themselves from, rather than integrating themselves with, the community. They often do not use local products or equipment, preventing the foreign investment "spill over" to improve the broader economy.

The Low-Wage Game

If these programs are not developing the Caribbean and Central American economies, why is the federal government pursuing them? According to the Labor Fund's Kernaghan and Steve Hellinger, executive director of the Development GAP, an international development nonprofit, the U.S. government encouraged such programs to help corporations gain access to lower wages both abroad and at home.

"Our report breaks down the myth about AID," says Kernaghan. "The government said it was to develop the region, to create jobs, to create democracy. They lied. They did this stuff to give U.S. companies access to low wages. Period. Now the government is finally admitting it."

AID and other programs are the latest steps in a long-term process of corporations relocating south. "You have to remember that this was a Reagan/Bush strategy. They had corporate support and a corporate agenda," says Hellinger. "This is only the latest round of support for the movement of investors from the North to the South to reduce costs and substantially increase their leverage with U.S. unions." Lower wages also keep corporations competitive with the Asian apparel industry which uses cheap, sometimes prison, labor.

The NLC found that to help U.S. businesses carry out the low-wage strategy, the U.S. government subsidizes financing, technical assistance, and worker retraining programs for companies who relocate to these zones.

AID supports promotional offices in the United States for at least 11 Central American and Caribbean countries. The goal of those offices is to: (1) sell U.S. companies on their countries' low wages, weak or unenforced health and safety rules, anti-union policies, and "adaptable" workers; (2) dole out U.S.-backed aid; and (3) assist companies in setting up new factories, many of which U.S. monies financed.

During the investigation, Kernaghan, along with a business-man friend of his, posed as the owners and managers of New Age Textiles, a small private company that produced 100 percent natural cotton reusable canvas bags. As a company willing to relocate, New Age Textiles attended trade shows, met with staff of promotion offices, and traveled to Honduras and El Salvador to probe into these programs and investigate reports of union-busting and poor working conditions.

When New Age "owners" visited an apparel trade show in April 1991, they discovered that the U.S. government employees, who work in the promotional offices, were quick to sell them on the advantages of moving offshore. "Even we were surprised," wrote the NLC about visiting an investment promotions booth for Jamaica. "Within a matter of minutes, we were approached by a Mr. Stuart Anderson who immediately began pitching New Age Textiles on the advantages of moving offshore to Jamaica." Anderson is an AID employee.

And the advantages to moving were many. In El Salvador, for example, AID spent $32 million to finance the start-up costs of constructing 129 factory buildings in new industrial parks. These factories now house companies, including many apparel manufacturers, targeting the U.S. market. AID also allowed El Salvador to use $5 million of U.S. Food for Peace aid to build a 72,000 square-foot factory in the San Bartolo Free Trade Zone. According to the NLC, it is now housing a formerly U.S.-based manufacturer.

AID created the Foundation of Entrepreneurs for Educational Development to help train the largely unskilled Salvadoran workforce for its new employers. To date, AID has granted the foundation $27 million. U.S. firms relocating to El Salvador can obtain a 50 percent subsidy to cover worker training costs. AID also established a $15 million line of credit for some export companies.

U.S. taxpayer money also provided assistance to El Salvador's

Ministry of Foreign Trade to help revise laws and regulations affecting exporters. Perhaps as a result, El Salvador developed a "Foreign Investment Incentive Package": 100 percent exemption from corporate income tax, import and export duties, and dividend and equity taxes. In addition, the United States has special tariff codes to benefit export-zone products.

The lack of unions, accompanied by computerized union blacklisting, also draws companies to the export zones. Blacklistings, torture, and killings of union leaders and members are prevalent in the Caribbean basin, particularly in El Salvador, Guatemala, and Honduras. When New Age Textiles visited Honduras, no one, from AID employees to export zone managers, hesitated in discussing union blacklisting, even though such actions violate U.S. trade laws, including the Caribbean Basin Initiative.

The manager of the INHDELVA Export Processing Zone (a zone where Van Heusen and Oshkosh B'Gosh have plants) told New Age that its computerized zone blacklist includes the names of all workers dismissed for any reason from any zone in the country. "We check it out [the list of job applicants] and will see problems with union members or anything like that," said the manager. "We tell you, okay, you have to get rid of this one or you have to get rid of that one."

Closing Shop

According to the Bureau of Labor Statistics, in 1992 the U.S. apparel and textile industries accounted for over 9 percent of all manufacturing jobs. The industries employed more production workers than the steel and auto industries combined.

But plant closings have decimated these industries. Perry Manufacturing—a maker of women's apparel sold by J.C. Penney, WalMart, K-Mart, and other national chain stores—moved to El Salvador with the help of FUSADES, El Salvador's AID-funded investment promotion organization. FUSADES secured Perry's factory space in the San Bartolo zone and arranged a start-up loan drawn from an AID-funded credit line. The U.S.

Overseas Private Investment Corporation insured Perry's Salvador investment with over $1 million in coverage.

The Perry move cost the United States the AID funds plus close to 1,500 apparel jobs. Three hundred and six of those jobs were lost at the Decaturville Sportswear company in Tennessee, which shut down in May 1991, despite, as plant manager Collins Pratt told a reporter, showing "an acceptable degree of profit." Unemployment in the county doubled following the plant closing, reaching almost 22 percent in July of that year. Some of those laid off had worked for the company for 25 years.

In a particularly nasty twist, workers at the Decaturville plant had been video-taped repairing faulty garments made at Perry's Salvadoran operation for six months prior to the plant closing. The company used the videos as training films in El Salvador.

Imports from Central America and the Caribbean have exploded since Reagan introduced the CBI in the early 1980s. Between 1980 and 1991, says the NLC, Caribbean Basin apparel imports increased 690 percent. In 1980, the domestic apparel industry produced 70 percent of all apparel purchased in the United States; today half comes from imports.

Plant closings translate into fewer jobs, devastated communities and lower wages. Competition from workers earning pennies per hour, plus the pressure of layoffs and plant closings, have driven real wages down 17 percent in the U.S. apparel industry.

U.S. women, especially women of color, are the big losers in the low-wage bidding game. Each year from 1979 to 1992 an average of 41,000 apparel workers in the United States lost their jobs. Three-quarters of U.S. apparel workers are women, over a third of whom are minorities. This combination makes them the U.S.'s most vulnerable workers.

Women apparel workers in the U.S., who on average earn $13,000 a year, must compete with poor young women workers in Central America. In Guatemala, those workers take home less than $600 a year.

Many export-zone companies hire only women. A survey by

the Honduran Committee for the Defense of Human Rights (CODEH) found that 95 percent of that country's export zone workers were women, the majority under 18 years of age. Export-zone companies hire young women because they can pay them less and believe they are more 'docile'.

The Untold Story of the 1980s

More than 200 export processing zones operate in 20 Central American and Caribbean countries. They house 3,000 manufacturing plants, employ 735,000 workers, and produce $14 billion in annual exports to the United States.

The Congressional mandate behind the AID program has a lofty goal: "To help the poor majority of people in developing countries... satisfy their basic needs and lead lives of decency, dignity, and hope." But CODEH, when it surveyed and heard testimony from Honduran free-zone employees, did not find that zone jobs provided for basic needs or allowed the women to lead lives of dignity and hope.

• Base pay for a 44-hour work week is $22.30. Most employees report working 10 hour days and averaging 10 hours of overtime. For a 54-hour week, the workers receive $24.60.

• One hundred percent of the workers report they must work "extremely hard" to keep up their quota assignments. There are various punishments for not fulfilling one's quota.

• One hundred percent of the women complained of eye irritations, skin rashes, nausea, headaches and coughs caused by airborne contaminants in the factory.

The Honduran Committee also heard of horrific working conditions. One woman told them about a room next to the personnel office that the plant supervisors "have used to beat the operators without anyone knowing it." Supervisors sexually abuse the women workers. If a worker won't let a supervisor fondle her, or if she does not move quickly enough, she is forced to lift a bench and hold it over her head for three hours without letting it fall. Managers will grab a worker by the back of the head and smash her face against a sewing machine.

Uncovering export-zone working conditions is difficult. Many zones and companies refuse entrance to visitors, including the country's own labor and health inspectors. Kurt Peterson, author of *The Maquiladora Revolution in Guatemala*, interviewed workers and heard how in some factories workers collapse from exhaustion and dehydration—because the factories are so hot, and the companies deny workers breaks and restrict access to drinking water.

Workers in both the United States and the Caribbean Basin have lost because of programs run by AID. U.S. workers have lost jobs and taken wage cuts. Central American workers gained sweatshop jobs instead of ones that would provide them with "dignity and hope."

And all of this, says Hellinger, is but the tip of the iceberg. "The United States," he says, "both directly and through international agencies such as the World Bank, has pushed economic policies in over 70 Third World countries that enable U.S. companies to take advantage of poor, unorganized workers." How these policies have wreaked havoc on these countries is the great untold story of the 1980s, he believes.

Demise of a Corporate Town
Jody A. Wright

Flint, Michigan

When General Motors began losing market share in the late 1970s, my father was among the first to be laid off. When you get laid off in Flint, there is quite literally nothing you can do: all the jobs have something to do with GM, and they aren't hiring. I remember how humiliated my father was waiting in line for unemployment checks ... and I remember how often my parents fought. It hurt both of them to tell us that we wouldn't get much for Christmas.

Why would anyone choose to remain in such a hopeless situation? The best answer is that many GM workers have no choice. Most are trained for labor no longer in demand, and they own houses they can't sell. No one wants to move into an area of high unemployment, high crime and few opportunities. For people like my father, whose GM roots go back two generations, it makes more sense to stick it out than to try to move away. It is not difficult to understand why these people do not get excited about the new jobs free trade is supposed to provide.

GM, by virtue of the high wages it offered in its flush times, attained a power over Flint and its residents that no person, let alone a corporation, ought to enjoy over any other person or group. GM can leave Flint whenever it likes, but the people of Flint cannot leave GM, not now nor in the near future.

Not long ago, a city just south of Flint persuaded GM to keep the local Chevy factory open with a series of tax breaks; GM accepted the handouts, then moved the plant to Mexico a few years later.

Stable jobs, extended families—everything that made Flint a banal but decent, democratic, deeply American place to live—are being pried from our grip in exchange for the tangible munificence provided by "market forces." But we should be constantly aware of the price we are being asked to pay. It remains to be seen how much longer Americans can worship at the altar of commerce and still sustain the illusion that our social life has not become pathologically greedy, uprooted and empty.

Excerpted from "End Game," In These Times, February 21, 1994.

11

Shattered Promises: The Truth Behind NAFTA's Claims of Job Creation

Peter Cooper and Lori Wallach

This chapter examines whether NAFTA has created the U.S. jobs that its proponents promised. During the NAFTA debate in 1993, the trade agreement's proponents used various economic models to promise remarkable gains for American workers. By tracking the specific job creation and export expansion promises of pro-NAFTA businesses and organizations, this report documents a broad sample of NAFTA's actual effects on U.S. jobs and our economy.

Our organization, Public Citizen, was able to identify more than 80 specific promises from pro-NAFTA business and government reports and Congressional testimony. As leading promoters of NAFTA, these were the firms most likely to embody the promised success of NAFTA. This report reveals how the real life experiences of these pro-NAFTA companies 20 months into NAFTA now embody a very different story—one that shows NAFTA isn't working.

Public Citizen tried to contact each of the companies for which we were able to find a specific NAFTA jobs or exports promise. We conducted an extensive investigation of the following sources to locate specific promises: the state-by-state NAFTA reports of USA*NAFTA and the National Association of Manufacturers (NAFTA's biggest boosters); the U.S. Department of Commerce's state-by-state reports; and the reams of Congressional testimony on NAFTA.

In the first weeks of August 1995, we conducted interviews with the identified companies in conjunction with *The Multinational Monitor*, an international news magazine published by Essential Information, Inc. These interviews document that the vast majority of specific company promises have not come close to fulfillment. Interviewers found that company after company conceded that they are nowhere close to realizing their predictions. A few firms have approached their promised goals of increased jobs and/or exports.

Our research reveals:

• 59 of 66 company-specific promises made by NAFTA advocates have been broken: The promises did not even come close to being fulfilled. That is, 89 percent of the companies that we contacted had not made any significant steps towards fulfilling their promises of U.S. job creation or export expansion.

• 90 percent of the NAFTA advocates' promises to increase U.S. jobs (46 of 51) have been broken; 87 percent of the promises to increase U.S. exports (13 of 15) have been broken.

• Only 7 of the 65 promises were "on target" to meet their promises — a mere 11 percent of promises kept.

• The broken promises pervade American business and cut across regional and industrial sectoral lines.

• Companies' responses fell into three categories: (1) 7 companies that are on track with their pre-NAFTA promises; (2) 59 companies that have broken their promises; and (3) 15 companies that made significant promises, but were unwilling or unable to provide current data to our interviewers.

• Allied Signal, General Electric, Proctor and Gamble, Mattel, Scott Paper and Zenith all made specific promises to create jobs, and all have laid off workers because of NAFTA as certified by the U.S. Department of Labor's special NAFTA unemployment assistance program.

The study covers large companies and associations, including Eastman-Kodak, Zenith, Polaroid, Sara Lee, the California

Tomato Board, Honeywell, Johnson & Johnson, Mattel, Petroleum Equipment Suppliers Association, Scott Paper and Xerox; medium size companies like Air-Hydraulics of Jackson, Mississippi and Pacer Corporation of Custer, South Dakota; and small companies like Canchola Foods of Nogales, Arizona and Orchard Heights Winery of Salem, Oregon.

Our report examines every promise of a pro-NAFTA company made in published materials that we could locate. We did not focus on the 578 firms in 48 states where workers have filed petitions with the Department of Labor as having lost their jobs due to NAFTA. However, to the extent that one of the companies making a specific promise is now listed on the Labor Department's NAFTA Trade Adjustment Assistance (NAFTA TAA) job loss list, we note it.

As of mid-August, 1995, the U.S. Department of Labor had certified 38,148 workers as having lost their jobs to NAFTA. A total of 68,482 workers have filed to receive NAFTA-related unemployment assistance through the NAFTA-TAA program. These numbers represent only the tip of the iceberg of NAFTA job losses because the NAFTA-TAA program is only available to some workers in some industries, and many workers file for assistance under other, better known and less complicated trade unemployment assistance programs.

It is especially revealing to discover the names of companies that stood to gain the most from NAFTA, the ones that were to have been the NAFTA "poster firms," on the NAFTA-TAA list of firms that laid off workers due to NAFTA. Allied Signal, Scott Paper, Mattel, General Electric, Proctor and Gamble, and Zenith all promised to create jobs, and all have laid off workers because of NAFTA.

An example of this practice is Mattel, a toy manufacturer from El Segundo, California. In 1993, Mattel Vice-President Fermin Cuza testified before the Ways and Means' Subcommittee on Trade that NAFTA would create jobs and have "a very positive effect on more than 2,000 [Mattel] U.S. employees." Mattel spokesperson Karen Stewart now says it is "too soon to tell" if

NAFTA has created any new jobs at Mattel. The Labor Department's NAFTA Trade Adjustment Assistance program (NAFTA-TAA) has certified that 520 workers at Mattel's Fisher Price facility in Medina, New York were laid off because of NAFTA due to "increased company imports from Mexico."

The interviews contained in our study reveal the reality of NAFTA's effects on specific companies. For example, in 1993 Polaroid predicted that "NAFTA will increase U.S. and Mexican exports as well as jobs." In August 1995, however, company spokesman Greg Van was unable to say whether or not the firm increased U.S. or Mexican exports, or increased any jobs in either country because of NAFTA. Rather, he conceded that NAFTA had "no profound impact" on employment at Polaroid. A 1993 National Association of Manufacturers report projected that Xerox would increase purchases from U.S. suppliers, as well as increase U.S. employment associated with Mexican trade. Yet, when we talked to Xerox's manager of public relations, he said that while Xerox had increased its exports to Mexico by 25 percent, this increase had "no material effect" on employment at Xerox.

An example of a large organization that has broken its pre-NAFTA promises is the Petroleum Equipment Suppliers Association (PESA). In 1993, PESA member companies predicted their sales to Mexico would triple the first year of NAFTA, creating nearly 3,000 new union and non-union jobs in the U.S. oil and gas equipment and service industries. However, according to Sherry Stevens, PESA's president, sales to Mexico have actually decreased 19 percent since 1993. Stevens conceded that NAFTA has not resulted in the creation of any new U.S. jobs by PESA members.

Air-Hydraulics Inc. is an example of a medium-sized firm that has been unable to come close to the pre-NAFTA promises of job creation. In 1993, company representatives predicted that "NAFTA could increase Air-Hydraulics business by 50 percent, adding 10 new jobs." Nevertheless, according to company President Joe Miller, [because of the peso devaluation] "we haven't been able to increase business. NAFTA looked very promising, but now we can't tell if we were right or wrong." Miller said the firm's sales to Mexico have decreased, and are at "pre-NAFTA levels."

Orchard Heights Winery of Salem, Oregon is an example of a small company that could not deliver on its NAFTA promises. A 1993 USA*NAFTA report promised that Orchard Heights would increase its exports to Mexico as tariffs on wine dropped from 20 percent to 10 percent, and transportation costs dropped from $20 a case to $10 a case by January 1994. Co-owner J. Eduardo Lopez predicted that "by 1994, we will be selling 4,000 to 5,000 cases to Mexico." Unfortunately, under the lower peso-dollar exchange rate, all NAFTA tariff reduction were effectively eliminated and the real price of potential exports rose above pre-NAFTA levels. Thus, according to Mr. Lopez, the company has "stopped exporting to Mexico," resulting in the loss of one full-time and seven part-time jobs.

In November 1993, President Clinton predicted that "if this trade agreement (NAFTA) passes, we estimate America will add another 200,000 jobs by 1995 alone." However, the economic models used by the Administration and the pro-NAFTA lobby to sell NAFTA to the American public, including the so-called "Hufbauer-Schott model," were methodologically flawed. As our study reveals, these flawed predictions have no relation to the present reality. By the same token, NAFTA's promoters—both inside and outside the Administration—predicted that by the end of 1995 the U.S. would enjoy a $9 billion trade surplus with Mexico. The reality is that the post-NAFTA surge in imports from Mexico resulted in an $8.6 billion trade deficit with Mexico, for just the first six months of 1995.

By adding the Mexican trade deficit numbers to our current deficit with Canada, our other NAFTA partner, the overall U.S. NAFTA trade deficit for the first six months of 1995 alone is $16.7 billion. By way of comparison, using actual Department of Commerce trade data in the formula used by NAFTA proponents used to predict job gains (whereby each billion dollars of net exports translates into 19,000 jobs), the real accumulated NAFTA trade deficit would translate into over three hundred thousand U.S. jobs *lost* in the first half of 1995 alone.

It is necessary to examine NAFTA's real-life effects to determine the best future course for our economic relations in the region. It is only prudent to consider carefully the real-life effects of NAFTA before considering any NAFTA expansion. Unless the evidence can support the promises of NAFTA supporters of job creation, higher wages and other broad economic and social benefits, the most appropriate future NAFTA discussion will be how to renegotiate a pact that might deliver on these promises.

If NAFTA in real life is undermining U.S. economic and social interests and those in the region, it must be renegotiated or terminated, not expanded. At a minimum, NAFTA's actual effect should be to cause no additional economic or social pain as compared to the *status quo ante* for the region. Unfortunately, our findings show that in reality, NAFTA is not creating the promised new jobs but is costing existing U.S. jobs. With the agreement heading in a direction exactly opposite of its promise, continuing on the current NAFTA path can only cause more problems.

To order copies of the full report, send a check or money order for $10, payable to Public Citizen, to: Public Citizen Publications, 1600 20th Street NW, Washington, DC 20009.

12

Corporate Technology and the Threat to Civil Society

Jeremy Rifkin

The global economy is undergoing a fundamental transformation in the nature of work brought on by the new technologies of the Information Age revolution. These profound technological and economic changes will force every country to rethink long-held assumptions about the nature of politics and citizenship.

At the heart of this historic shift are sophisticated computers, robotics, telecommunications and other Information Age technologies that are fast replacing human beings, especially in the manufacturing sector. The number of factory workers in the United States has declined from 33 percent of the workforce to under 17 percent in the past thirty years, even as U.S. companies have continued to increase output and overall production, maintaining our country's position as the number-one manufacturing power in the world.

For most of the 1980s it was fashionable to blame foreign competition and cheap labor markets abroad for the loss of manufacturing jobs in the United States. In some industries, especially the garment trade and electronics, that has been the case. Recently, however, economists have begun to revise their views. Paul Krugman of Stanford and Robert Lawrence of Harvard suggest, on the basis of extensive data, that "the concern, widely voiced during the 1950s and 1960s, that industrial workers would lose their jobs because of automation, is closer to the truth than the current preoccupation with a presumed loss of manufacturing jobs because of foreign competition."

Automated technologies have been reducing the need for human labor in every manufacturing category. By the year 2005, less than 12 percent of the U.S. workforce will be on the factory floor, and by the year 2020, less than 2 percent of the entire global workforce will still be engaged in factory work. Over the next 25 years we will see the virtual elimination of the blue-collar, mass assembly-line worker from the production process.

Until recently, economists and politicians assumed that displaced factory workers would find new jobs in the service sector. Now, however, the service sector is also beginning to automate: In the banking, insurance and wholesale and retail sectors, companies are eliminating layer after layer of management and infrastructure, replacing the traditional corporate pyramid and mass white-collar workforces with small, highly skilled professional work teams, using state-of-the-art software and telecommunications technologies. Even those companies that continue to use large numbers of white-collar workers have changed the conditions of employment, transferring workers from permanent jobs to "just in time" employment, including leased, temporary and contingent work, in an effort to reduce wage and benefit packages, cut labor costs and increase profit margins.

Acknowledging that both the manufacturing and service sectors are quickly re-engineering their infrastructures and automating their production processes, many mainstream economists and politicians have pinned their hopes on new job opportunities along the information superhighway and in cyberspace. Although the "knowledge sector" will create some new jobs, they will be too few to absorb the millions of workers displaced by the new technologies. That's because the knowledge sector is, by nature, an elite and not a mass workforce. Indeed, the shift from mass to elite labor is what distinguishes work in the Information Age from that in the Industrial Age.

With near-workerless factories and virtual companies already looming on the horizon, every nation will have to grapple with the question of what to do with the millions of people whose labor is needed less, or not at all, in an ever-more-automated global economy. While mainstream Democrats and Republicans have embraced the Information Age, extolling the virtues of cyberspace and virtual reality, they have, for the most part, refused to address the question of how to insure that the gains of the high-tech global economy will be shared. Up to now, those productivity gains have been used primarily to enhance corporate profits, to the exclusive benefit of stockholders, top corporate managers and the emerging elite of high-tech knowledge workers. If that trend continues, the widening gap between the haves and have-nots is likely to lead to social unrest and more crime and violence. Millions of middle-class and working-class Americans, worried about their own eroding economic fortunes, including loss of job security and falling real wages, may become easy prey to the nascent fascist rhetoric of the extreme right. The politics of scapegoating is already in ascendance, as right-wing politicians blame affirmative action programs, feminists, illegal aliens and immigrants, cheap labor abroad, the "international banking conspiracy" and the United Nations for the deepening economic malaise.

The antidote to the politics of paranoia and hate is an open and sober discussion about the underlying technological and economic forces that are leading to increased productivity on the one hand and a diminishing need for mass labor on the other. That discussion needs to be accompanied by a bold new social vision that can speak directly to the challenges facing us. In short, we need to begin thinking seriously about what a radically different society might look like in an ever more automated global economy.

In the past, when new technologies dramatically increased productivity, U.S. workers sought a share of the productivity gains and organized collectively to demand a shorter workweek and better pay and benefits. Today, instead of reducing the workweek, employers are reducing the workforce. The new labor-saving technologies of the Information Age should be used to free us for greater leisure, not less pay and growing underemployment. Of course, employers argue that shortening the workweek and sharing the productivity gains with workers will be too costly and will threaten their ability to compete both domestically and abroad. That need not be so. Companies like Hewlett-Packard in France and BMW in Germany have reduced their workweek from thirty-seven to thirty-one hours while continuing to pay workers at the thirty-seven-hour rate. In return, the workers have agreed to work in shifts. The companies reasoned that if they could keep the new high-tech plants operating on a twenty-four-hour basis they could double or triple productivity and thus afford to pay workers more for working less time.

In France, government officials are considering offering to rescind payroll taxes for the employer if management voluntarily reduces the workweek. While the government will lose tax revenue, economists argue that it will make up the difference in other ways. With a reduced workweek more people will be working and fewer will be on welfare. And the new workers will buy goods and pay taxes, all of which will benefit employers, the economy and the government.

In the United States, the federal government ought to consider extending tax credits to any company willing to do three things: voluntarily reduce its workweek; implement a profit-sharing plan so that its employees will benefit directly from the productivity gains; and agree to a formula by which compensation to top management and shareholder dividends are not disproportionate to the benefits distributed to the rest of the company's workforce. With such an incentive, employers would be more inclined to make the transition, especially if it gave them a marked advantage over their competitors.

Two powerful forces increase the likelihood of a new accommodation between U.S. management and the workforce. While reducing the labor component in the production process often translates into short-term gains for each company, employers are beginning to see a troubling decline in consumer purchasing power. As more and more workers are placed in temporary, part-time and contingent employment and experience a decline in wages, purchasing power diminishes. Even those workers with permanent jobs find their wages and benefits falling. The quickened pace of corporate re-engineering, technological displacement and declining income can be seen in stagnant inventories and sluggish growth, which in turn set off a new spiral of reengineering, technology displacement and wage cuts, further fueling the downward drift in consumption.

The second Achilles heel for employers in the emerging Information Age—and one rarely talked about—is the effect on capital accumulation when vast numbers of employees are reduced to temporary work and part-time assignments, or let go altogether, so that employers can avoid paying out benefits, especially pension-fund benefits. As it turns out, pension funds, now worth more than $5 trillion in the United States alone, have served as a forced savings pool that has financed capital investments for more than forty years. In 1992, pension funds accounted for 74 percent of net individual savings, more than one-third of all corporate equities and nearly 40 percent of all corporate bonds. Pension assets exceed the assets of commercial banks and make up nearly one-third of the total financial assets of the U.S. economy. In 1993, pension funds made new investments of between $1 trillion and $1.5 trillion. If companies continue to marginalize their workforces and let large numbers of employees go, the capitalist system will slowly collapse on itself as it is drained of the pension funds necessary for new capital investments.

A steady loss of consumer purchasing power and a decline in workers' pension-fund capital are likely to have a significant impact on the long-term health of the economy. Even an "enlightened" management is unlikely to heed the warning signals without pressure being brought to bear from both inside and outside the companies. The thirty-hour workweek ought to become a rallying cry for millions of U.S. workers. Shorter workweeks and better pay and benefits were the benchmarks for measuring the success of the Industrial Age in the past century. We should demand no less of the Information Age in the coming century.

Even with a much-reduced workweek, the United States and every other nation is still going to have to address the problem of finding alternative forms of work for the millions of people who are no longer needed to produce goods and services for an increasingly automated market economy. Up to now, the marketplace and government have been looked to, almost exclusively, for solutions to the growing economic crisis. Today, with the market economy less able to provide permanent jobs and with the government retreating from its traditional role of employer of last resort, the nation's civil sector may be the best hope for absorbing the millions of displaced workers.

While politicians traditionally divide the United States into a spectrum running from the marketplace on one side to the government on the other, it is more accurate to think of society as a three-legged stool made up of the market sector, the government sector and the civil sector. The first leg creates market capital the second leg creates public capital and the third leg creates social capital. Of the three legs, the oldest and most important, but least acknowledged, is the civil sector.

For more than 200 years, this sector has helped shape the American experience. The nation's schools and colleges, its hospitals, social-service organizations, fraternal orders, women's clubs, youth organizations, civil rights groups, social justice organizations, environmental protection groups, animal welfare organizations, theaters, orchestras, art galleries, libraries, museums, civic associations, community development organizations, neighborhood advisory councils, volunteer fire departments and civilian security patrols are all part of the Third Sector.

There are currently more than 1.4 million nonprofit organizations in the United States, with total combined assets of more than $500 billion. Nonprofit activities run the gamut from social services to health care, education and research, the arts, religion and advocacy. The expenditures of America's nonprofit organizations exceed the gross domestic product of all but seven nations in the world. The civil society already contributes more than 6 percent of America's G.D.P., and is responsible for 10.5 percent of total employment. More people are employed in Third Sector organizations than work in the construction, electronics, transportation or textile and apparel industries.

The opportunity now exists to create millions of new jobs in the civil society. But freeing up the labor and talent of men and women no longer needed in the market and government sectors for the creation of social capital in neighborhoods and communities will cost money. The logical source for this money is the new Information Age economy; we should tax a percentage of the wealth generated by the new high-tech marketplace and redirect it into the creation of jobs in the nonprofit sector and the rebuilding of the social commons. This new agenda represents a powerful countervailing force to the new global marketplace.

In the old scheme of things, finding the proper balance between the market and government dominated political discussion. In the new scheme, finding a balance among the market, government and civil sector becomes paramount. Since the civil society relies on both the market and government for its survival and well-being, its future will depend, in large part, on the creation of a new social force that can make demands on both the market and government sectors to pump some of the vast financial gains of the new Information Age economy into the creation of social capital.

This third force in U.S. political life exists but has not yet been galvanized into a mainstream social movement. It consists of the 89 million Americans—one out of every two adults—who give an average of four hours or more of their time each week to serve in the nonprofit organizations that make up the sprawling civil society. Third Sector participants come from every race and ethnic background, and from every class and walk of life. They are Republicans, Democrats and Independents. The one thing they share is a belief in the importance of service to the community and the creation of social capital. If that powerful shared value can be transformed into a sense of common purpose and identity, we could redraw the political map.

There are signs of that beginning to happen. In cities and towns all over the country, civic organizations are joining together, many for the first time, to address the economic and social issues facing their communities. They are asking tough questions about the allocation of scarce economic resources and beginning to grapple with the very difficult issues of how to restore the work life and civic life of their communities.

While public advocacy groups have long played this role in the Third Sector—cajoling, pressuring and at times actively opposing powerful economic and political forces in their own communities—what's new in the equation is the involvement of heretofore apolitical groups: fraternal, service, religious, educational and artistic. Feeling the pressure of both market constriction and government retrenchment, civic organizations are becoming increasingly worried about the very survival of the civil society. Their growing concerns are leading some of them to become more involved in collective efforts to solve community-wide problems.

It's too early to predict whether these fledgling efforts will blossom into a mature social movement. What can be said is that seeds are being sown in communities across the country for the rebirth of the civil society as a powerful force in American life.

There is much to be gained from the shift in political perspective away from the old polar model of market versus government to the new tripartite model of market, government and civil sectors. For example, consider the fortunes of four traditional constituencies—people of color, labor, women and environmentalists—in the new tripartite politics. People of color continue to be the primary victims of the revolutionary changes taking place in the nature of work. Technology displacement has affected African-Americans and other minorities in disproportionate numbers. According to a report issued by the Equal Employment Opportunity Commission, black wage-earners made up nearly one-third of the 180,000 manufacturing jobs lost in 1990 and 1991. Blacks also suffered disproportionately in the loss of white-collar and service jobs in the early 1990s. The reason for the heavy losses in black employment, according to *The Wall Street Journal*, is that "more than half of all black workers held positions in the four job categories where companies made net employment cuts: office and clerical, skilled, semi-skilled and laborers." Taxing a portion of the productivity gains of the new Information Age economy and allocating those funds to the creation of jobs and infrastructure in the civil sector is essential if we are to reverse the downward spiral of minority groups in America.

Organized labor's hopes also rest, in part, on the emergence of civil society as a new social force. Unions are finding it more difficult to recruit workers in the new economy. Organizing at the point of production becomes difficult, and often impossible, when dealing with temporary, leased, contingent and part-time workers and the growing number of telecommuters. At the same time, the strike is becoming increasingly irrelevant in an age of automated production processes. Joining with Third Sector organizations—service, fraternal, civic and advocacy—to exert a collective "geographic" pressure on management to share some of the gains of the Information Age with workers and local communities may be labor's best hope for success in the new era.

Although the new economy is going to bring a fundamental shift in gender roles, with more women working in the marketplace and more men at home and in the community, women are still likely to remain the primary advocates of social capital because of their long-standing relationship to the Third Sector. Women have been the mainstay of the civil society for more than 200 years, volunteering their time to create the social capital of the country. Their contribution has gone largely unnoticed, in part because the political importance of social capital has gone largely unheralded. By politicizing the social commons, elevating the importance of social capital and making demands on the new Information Age economy to pump some of the gains into the civil society, women could help create a new third force in American politics as we enter a new century.

Environmentalists also have much to gain from elevating the role of the Third Sector and making social capital equal in importance to market and public capital. The environmental community is currently involved in a debate on how to convince consumers to simplify their life-styles in order to preserve the earth's dwindling resources and promote a sustainable economy. Unfortunately, as long as most people's primary identity is with the marketplace, the values of expanded production and unlimited consumption will continue to influence personal behavior. On the other hand it is likely that the more time Americans spend in the Third Sector, as both paid employees and volunteers, the less consumer-oriented they will be, for the simple reason that personal relationships and community bonds will replace shopping as a life-fulfilling experience. Of the three forms of capital, social capital is the most environmentally benign. Unlike market or public capital, which use large amounts of the earth's resources, social capital uses relatively few resources, relying almost exclusively on the few thousand calories of energy each person requires daily to maintain a healthy mind and body.

The problem of rising productivity in the face of declining wages and vanishing jobs is likely to be one of the defining issues around the world in the years ahead. Growing social unrest and increasing political destabilization arising from this historic shift in work is forcing activists of every persuasion, as well as politicians and political parties, to search for a "radical new center" that speaks to the concerns and aspirations of a majority of the electorate. The conventional political discussion continues to take place along the polar spectrum of marketplace versus government—a playing field that is increasingly limited. Redirecting the political debate to a tripartite model—with civil society centered between the market and government—will fundamentally change the nature of political discourse and open up the possibility of re-envisioning politics, the economy and the nature of work and society.

Reprinted with permission from *The Nation* magazine. © The Nation Company, L.P.

Mother Earth and the Corporate Imperative

Anyone who is reasonably well-informed knows that there are very serious threats to our environment that are getting worse each year. The ozone layer that protects all living things from harmful ultraviolet rays is eroding at an accelerating rate. The world's water sources are being threatened by pollution and overuse. Forests are being cut down at an unsustainable rate. Air pollution in major cities is shortening the lives of millions of people and lowering the productivity of many more. All of these threats are made worse by the fact that global corporations have the size and flexibility to resist government efforts to limit environmental damage. Many government leaders are either bought off or intimidated by corporate threats to leave the local economy, taking much-needed jobs with them.

Whatever Americans may think about third world poverty and the suffering of people outside our border, these environmental trends pose a threat to everyone, irrespective of national boundaries. In his essay, "Global Ecology and the Common Good," John Bellamy Foster dissects the "treadmill of production" and how its money values push us in a direction opposed to the basic ecological cycles of the planet. In "NAFTA's Environmental Side Show," Andrew Wheat exposes how the North American Free Trade Agreement (NAFTA) is failing to keep increased cross-border trade and investment from destroying the environment. Jean Anne Casey and Colleen Hobbs, in "Look What the GATT Dragged In," show how the General Agreement on Tariffs and Trade (GATT) has opened the United States up to some rather strange environmental problems. Norman Solomon shows in

"Shrugging Off an Attack on the Clean Air Act" that the World Trade Organization is already showing its potential for undermining environmental safeguards that took years of citizen organizing to establish.

Global Ecology and the Common Good

John Bellamy Foster

Over the course of the twentieth century, human population has increased more than threefold and gross world product perhaps twentyfold. Such expansion has placed increasing pressure on the ecology of the planet. Everywhere we look—in the atmosphere, oceans, watersheds, forests, soil, etc.— it is now clear that rapid ecological decline is setting in.[1]

Faced with the frightening reality of global ecological crisis, many are now calling for a moral revolution that would incorporate ecological values into our culture. This demand for a new ecological morality is, I believe, the essence of Green thinking. The kind of moral transformation envisaged is best captured by Aldo Leopold's land ethic, which says we abuse land because we regard it as a commodity belonging to us. When we begin to see land as a community to which we belong, we may begin to use it with love and respect.

Yet behind most appeals to ecological morality there lies the presumption that we live in a society where the morality of the individual is the key to the morality of society. If people as individuals could simply change their moral stance with respect to nature and alter their behavior in areas such as propagation, consumption, and the conduct of business, all would be well.[2]

What is too often overlooked in such calls for moral transformation is the central institutional fact of our society: what might be called the global "treadmill of production." The logic of this treadmill can be broken down into six elements. First, built into this global system, and constituting its central rationale, is the increasing accumulation of wealth by a relatively small section of the population at the top of the social pyramid. Second, there is a long-term movement of workers away from self-employment and into wage jobs that are contingent on the continual expansion of production. Third, the competitive struggle between businesses necessitates on pain of extinction the allocation of accumulated wealth to new, revolutionary technologies that serve to expand production. Fourth, wants are manufactured in a manner that creates an insatiable hunger for more. Fifth, government becomes increasingly responsible for promoting national economic development, while ensuring some degree of "social security" for at least a portion of its citizens. Sixth, the dominant means of communication and education are part of the treadmill, serving to reinforce its priorities and values.[3]

A defining trait of the system is that it is a kind of giant squirrel cage. Everyone, or nearly everyone, is part of this treadmill and is unable or unwilling to get off. Investors and managers are driven by the need to accumulate wealth and to expand the scale of their operations in order to prosper within a globally competitive milieu. For the vast majority, the commitment to the treadmill is more limited and indirect: they simply need to obtain jobs at liveable wages. But to retain those jobs and to maintain a given standard of living in these circumstances it is necessary, like the Red Queen in *Through the Looking Glass,* to run faster and faster in order to stay in the same place.

In such an environment, as the nineteenth-century German philosopher Arthur Schopenhauer once said, "A man can do what he wants. But he can't want what he wants." Our wants are conditioned by the kind of society in which we live. Looked at in this way, it is not individuals acting in accordance with their own innate desires, but rather the treadmill of production on which we are all placed that has become the main enemy of the environment.[4]

Clearly, this treadmill leads in a direction that is incompat-
ible with the basic ecological cycles of the planet. A continuous
3 percent average annual rate of growth in industrial production,
such as obtained from 1970 to 1990, would mean that world industry would double in size every twenty-five years, grow
sixteenfold approximately every century, increase by 50 times
every two centuries, 4,000 times every three centuries, etc.. Further, the tendency of the present treadmill of production is to
expand the output of raw materials and energy because the greater
this flow—from extraction through the delivery of final products to consumers—the more opportunity there is to realize profits. In order to generate profits, the treadmill relies heavily on
energy-intensive, capital-intensive technology, which allows it
to economize on labor inputs. Yet increased output and more
substitution of energy and machines for labor mean a more rapid
depletion of high-quality energy sources and other natural resources, and a larger amount of wastes dumped into the environment. It is unlikely therefore that the world could sustain many
more doublings of industrial output under the present system
without experiencing a complete ecological catastrophe. Indeed,
we are already overshooting certain critical ecological thresh-
olds.[5]

Matters are made worse by the tendency in recent decades to
move from "gross insults" to the environment to "microtoxicity."
As synthetic products (like plastic) are substituted for natural
ones (like wood and wool), the older pollutants associated with
nineteenth-century industrialization are being replaced by more
hazardous pollutants such as those resulting from chlorine-re-
lated (organochlorine) production—the source of DDT, dioxin,
Agent Orange, PCBs, and CFCs. The degree of toxicity associated with a given level of output has thus risen fairly steadily
over the last half century.[6]

It would seem, then, that from an environmental perspective
we have no choice but to resist the treadmill of production. This
resistance must take the form of a far-reaching moral revolution.
In order to carry out such a moral transformation we must con-

front what the great American sociologist C. Wright Mills called "the higher immorality." The "higher immorality" for Mills was a "structural immorality" built into the institutions of power in our society—in particular the treadmill of production. "In a civilization so thoroughly business-penetrated as America," he wrote, money becomes "the one unambiguous marker of success . . . the sovereign American value." Such a society, dominated by the corporate rich with the support of the political power elite, is a society of "organized irresponsibility," where moral virtue is divorced from success, and knowledge from power. Public communication, rather than constituting the basis for the exchange of ideas necessary for the conduct of a democracy, is largely given over to "an astounding volume of propaganda for commodities . . . addressed more often to the belly or to the groin than to the head or the heart." The corrupting influence that all of this has on the general public is visible in the loss of the capacity for moral indignation, the growth of cynicism, a drop in political participation, and the emergence of a passive, commercially centered existence. In short, the higher immorality spells the annihilation of a meaningful moral and political community.[7]

Manifestations of this higher immorality—in which money divorced from all other considerations has become the supreme reality—are all around us. In 1992 alone U.S. business spent perhaps $1 trillion on marketing, simply convincing people to consume more and more goods. This exceeded by about $600 billion the amount spent on education—public and private—at all levels. Under these circumstances we can expect people to grow up with their heads full of information about saleable commodities, and empty of knowledge about human history, morality, culture, science, and the environment. What is most valued in such a society is the latest style, the most expensive clothing, the finest car. Hence, it is not surprising that more than 93 percent of teenage girls questioned in a survey conducted in the late 1980s indicated that their favorite leisure activity was to go shopping. Not long ago *Fortune* magazine quoted Dee Hock, former head of the Visa bank card operation, as saying, "It's not that people value money more but that they value everything else so much less—not that they are more greedy but that they have no other values to keep greed in check."

"Our social life is organized in such a way," German environmentalist Rudolf Bahro has observed, "that even people who work with their hands are more interested in a better car than in the single meal of the slum-dweller on the southern half of the earth or the need of the peasant there for water; or even a concern to expand their own consciousness, for their own self-realization."

Reflecting on the growing use of pesticides in our society, Rachel Carson wrote that this was indicative of "an era dominated by industry, in which the right to make money, at whatever cost to others, is seldom challenged."[8]

Given the nature of the society in which we live, one must therefore be wary of solutions to environmental problems that place too much emphasis on the role of individuals, or too little emphasis on the treadmill of production and the higher immorality that it engenders. To be sure, it is necessary for individuals to struggle to organize their lives so that in their consumption they live more simply and ecologically. But to lay too much stress on this alone is to place too much onus on the individual, while ignoring institutional facts. Alan Durning of the Worldwatch Institute, for example, argues that "we consumers have an ethical obligation to curb our consumption, since it jeopardizes the chances for future generations. Unless we climb down the consumption ladder a few rungs, our grandchildren will inherit a planetary home impoverished by our affluence."

This may seem like simple common sense but it ignores the higher immorality of a society like the United States in which the dominant institutions treat the public as mere consumers to be targeted with all of the techniques of modern marketing. The average adult in the United States watches 21,000 television commercials a year, about 75 percent of which are paid for by the 100 largest corporations. It also ignores the fact that the treadmill of production is rooted not in consumption but in production. Within the context of this system it is therefore economically naive to think that the problem can be solved simply by getting consumers to refrain from consumption and instead to save and invest their income. To invest means to expand the scale of productive capacity, increasing the size of the treadmill.[9]

Even more questionable are the underlying assumptions of those who seek to stop environmental degradation by appealing not to individuals in general but to the ethics of individuals at the top of the social pyramid and to corporations. Thus in his widely heralded book, *The Ecology of Commerce*, Paul Hawken argues for a new environmental ethic for businesspeople and corporations. After advocating an ambitious program for ecological change, Hawken states, "Nothing written, suggested, or proposed is possible unless business is willing to embrace the world we live within and lead the way." According to Hawken, "the ultimate purpose of business is not, or should not be, simply to make money. Nor is it merely a system of making and selling things. The promise of business is to increase the general well-being of humankind through service, a creative invention and ethical philosophy."

Thus he goes on to observe that, "If Dupont, Monsanto, and Dow believe they are in the synthetic chemical production business, and cannot change this belief, they and we are in trouble. If they believe they are in business to serve people, to help solve problems, to use and employ the ingenuity of workers to improve the lives of people around them by learning from the nature that gives us life, we have a chance."[10]

The central message here is that businesspeople merely have to change the ethical bases of their conduct and all will be well with the environment. Such views underestimate the extent to which the treadmill of production and the higher immorality are built into our society. Ironically, Hawken's argument places too much responsibility and blame on the individual corporate manager—since he or she too is likely to be a mere cog in the wheel of the system. As the great linguistics theorist and media critic Noam Chomsky has explained, "The chairman of the board will always tell you that he spends his every waking hour laboring so that people will get the best possible products at the cheapest possible price and work in the best possible conditions. But it is an institutional fact, independent of who the chairman of the board is, that he'd better be trying to maximize profit and market share, and if he doesn't do that, he's not going to be chairman of the board any more. If he were ever to succumb to the delusions that he expresses, he'd be out."[11]

To be successful within any sphere in this society generally means that one has thoroughly internalized those values associated with the higher immorality. There is, as economist John Kenneth Galbraith has pointed out, a "culture of contentment" at the top of the social hierarchy: those who benefit most from the existing order have the least desire for change.[12]

Resistance to the treadmill of production therefore has to come mainly from the lower echelons of society, and from social movements rather than individuals. This can only occur, to quote the late German Green Party leader Petra Kelly, if ecological concerns are "tied to issues of economic justice—the exploitation of the poor by the rich." Behind every environmental struggle of today there is a struggle over the expansion of the global treadmill—a case of landless workers or villagers who are compelled to destroy nature in order to survive, or of large corporations that seek to expand profits with little concern for the natural and social devastation that they leave in their wake. Ecological development is possible, but only if the economic as well as environmental injustices associated with the treadmill are addressed. An ecological approach to the economy is about having enough, not having more. It must have as its first priority people, particularly poor people, rather than production or even the environment, stressing the importance of meeting basic needs and long-term security. This is the common morality with which we must combat the higher immorality of the treadmill. Above all we must recognize the old truth, long understood by the romantic and socialist critics of capitalism, that increasing production does not eliminate poverty.[13]

Indeed, the global treadmill is so designed that the poor countries of the world often help finance the rich ones. During the period from 1982 to 1990, the Third World was a "net exporter of hard currency to the developed countries, on average $30 billion per year." In this same period Third World debtors remitted to their creditors in the wealthy nations an average of almost $12.5 billion per month in payments on debt alone. This is equal to what the entire Third World spends each month on health and education. It is this system of global inequity that reinforces both overpopulation (since poverty spurs population growth) and the kind of rapacious development associated with the destruction of tropical rain forests in the Third World.[14]

For those with a pragmatic bent, much of what I have said here may seem too global and too abstract. The essential point that I want to leave you with, however, is the notion that although we are all on the treadmill, we do not all relate to it in the same way and with the same degree of commitment. I have found in my research into the ancient forest struggle in the Northwest—and others have discovered the same thing in other settings—that ordinary workers have strong environmental values even though they may be at loggerheads with the environmental movement. In essence they are fighting for their lives and livelihoods at a fairly basic level.[15]

We must find a way of putting people first in order to protect the environment. There are many ways of reducing the economic stakes in environmental destruction on the part of those who have little direct stake in the treadmill itself. But this means taking seriously issues of social and economic inequality as well as environmental destruction. Only by committing itself to what is now called "environmental justice" (combining environmental concerns and social justice) can the environmental movement avoid being cut off from those classes of individuals who are most resistant to the treadmill on social grounds. The alternative is to promote an environmental movement that is very successful in creating parks with Keep Out! signs, yet is complicit with the larger treadmill of production. By recognizing that it is not people (as individuals and in aggregate) that are enemies of the environment but the historically specific economic and social order in which we live, we can find sufficient common ground for a true moral revolution to save the earth.

Who Is the Terminator?

Author Ziauddin Sardar decided to go to Sarawak, Malaysia, to find an "untouched" group of indigenous people.

After dark the first evening, everybody was sitting around and seemed to be feeling a little uncomfortable. Noticing this, Sardar asked through his guide whether they were upset by his presence and whether he should go and sleep somewhere else. The villagers replied, "Not at all," but they had become quite bored sitting around in the dark. The villagers wondered if Sardar would mind if they watched TV. So they went out and turned on the generator. After the lights came on, they found only an old BBC serial, which they had seen before, on TV. Then they pulled out the VCR and put a long scroll on the wall: a poster advertising Terminator II. They all sat and watched the video version of Terminator II. When it was over, Sardar asked what the film meant to the villagers. They said that the Terminator was like the tractors they now hear in the jungle. "They are getting closer and closer all the time and we know we are going to be overrun." The villagers had totally reframed the movie. As Sardar commented, "Terminator II was the Western model of development that was coming to overwhelm them."

Today, the ubiquitousness of this Western model is the driving issue for millions of citizen activists trying to limit its power and that of its corporate agents. The temptation and reach of this Western model, now dominating cultures all over the world, is provoking tremendous concern for culture and fueling the growth of grassroots globalism and the civil society.

From Hazel Henderson, Building a Win-Win World: Life Beyond Global Economic Warfare *(San Francisco: Berrett-Koehler Publishers, 1996), pp. 173-174.*

NAFTA's Environmental Side Show:

Andrew Wheat

As the North American Free Trade Agreement (NAFTA) completed its second year of implementation in January 1996, the environmental side agreement that President Bill Clinton negotiated to "fix" NAFTA's environmental deficiencies appeared to be falling short of the mark.

The side agreement, the North American Agreement on Environmental Cooperation, achieved its unofficial goal: to secure NAFTA support from some of the largest U.S. environmental groups (the National Wildlife Federation, the World Wildlife Fund, the Environmental Defense Fund, the Natural Resources Defense Council and the National Audubon Society) and to provide green cover to some members of Congress who wanted to vote for NAFTA while presenting themselves as environmentalists.

The side agreement has not been so successful in accomplishing its official goals through bodies such as the North American Commission on Environmental Cooperation (CEC). The side agreement established the CEC to secure effective enforcement of environmental laws and regulations, in part through a petition process open to non-governmental organizations. The CEC rejected two of the first three petitions it received. Its response to the third petition did not impress environmentalists.

Belly-Up Birds

The Commission's first citizen-initiated challenge addressed the mysterious deaths of between 20,000 to 40,000 birds in the

Silva Reservoir in the central Mexican state of Guanajuato in the winter of 1994-95. In June 1995, the Group of 100, an organization of environmentally minded artists and scientists from throughout the Americas, joined by the Mexican Center for Environmental Law and the U.S.-based National Audubon Society, petitioned the CEC Secretariat to investigate the bird deaths [see "Environment Tests NAFTA," *Multinational Monitor*, July/August 1995]. The reservoir, located 200 miles northwest of Mexico City in the Turbio River Basin, serves as a haven for migrating birds that spend warmer months in the United States and Canada. In mid-December 1994, local residents found thousands of dead and dying birds in the reservoir. After 20 species of birds— including ducks, egrets, ibis, black-necked stilts, sandpipers and American coots— perished, the Mexican government drained the reservoir.

Establishing the cause of the bird deaths has generated heated debate. Mexico's National Water Commission initially argued that a large, one-time dumping of the pesticide endosulfan by unknown parties was responsible for the deaths. Local environmentalists instead speculated that the bird deaths were caused by chromium pollution, a cause they said was overlooked to protect industry. Chromium is manufactured by a nearby chemical plant and is used by hundreds of local tanneries.

The Secretariat formed a tri-national scientific advisory panel in July 1995 to study the problem. The Secretariat's report, based on the panel's research, was released at an October 1995 meeting of the CEC Council of Ministers in Oaxaca, Mexico. The "over-riding cause of mortality of waterbirds at the Silva Reservoir was botulism; however, a small percentage of birds may have died of other causes," the report says. "The panel found that exposure to heavy metals, in particular chromium, lead and mercury, was indicated in some of the birds that the panel analyzed."

The Group of 100 criticized the report for downplaying the role of industrial toxins. "We are not terribly satisfied with the findings because they are weighted towards saying that the main cause of mortality was botulism," says Betty Ferber, international coordinator of the Group of 100.

National Audubon Society lawyer Mary Minette expressed overall satisfaction with the report's findings. But Minette also raised concerns about whether report recommendations—which included a suggestion to drain the reservoir immediately if evidence of another die-off appeared, and to alter the reservoir's topography to make it less conducive to botulism outbreaks—would be carried out and, if they were, whether they would prevent a recurrence of the tragedy.

A striking aspect of the report is how little of it— notwithstanding the report's general language encouraging the Mexican government to "implement a targeted pollution prevention program ... to decrease industrial pollution in a substantial way"—directly targets the sources of industrial and sewage pollution in the Silva Reservoir. This shortcoming is all the more notable in view of the report's conclusion that "while neither the panel nor the Secretariat examined regulatory and compliance issues, it is clear that the Turbio River Basin is a highly polluted ecosystem and that much effort is needed to ensure an important decrease of industrial pollution in the region."

Asked about the absence from the report of recommendations to aggressively reduce source pollution in the Turbio Basin, Andrew Hamilton, who heads the CEC's Science Division, says the panel limited its recommendations in deference to the Turbio Basin Initiative, a voluntary pollution reduction program launched by the Mexican government in February 1995. The panel viewed this initiative as a "pretty serious effort, at least on paper, to involve a broad coalition of stakeholders and to get some commitments on paper to reduce in a very substantive way both the industrial and the municipal sewage coming into that system."

Hamilton says the panel identified two options. "We could spend a lot of our effort looking for which particular industry contributed the most chromium into the system, when we really couldn't say definitely that chromium was the cause of the problem. We felt that, in the long haul, we would gain more by emphasizing the need to hold them to their commitments on [the Turbio Basin Initiative] and work hard to implement this rather ambitious initiative, given the scale of things in that part of the world," he says. "I think that, without a lot of encouragement, that [the Turbio Basin Initiative] will fade back, and this [the panel's recommendations] may fade too."

U.S. Environmental Laxity I: Endangered Species

In promoting the environmental side agreement, President Bill Clinton cited the need to promote "procedural safeguards and remedies that we take for granted in our country," and to "give citizens the right to challenge objectionable environmental practices by the Mexicans or Canadians." Clinton did not foresee the need for the side agreement to ensure environmental protection in the United States. Yet, the second and third petitions filed with the CEC pressed grievances against some environmentally hostile policies of a Republican-dominated U.S. Congress. The Republican initiatives that have been the subject of CEC petitions are efforts to weaken the Endangered Species Act (ESA) and to increase logging on federal lands, especially in the northwest United States. In contrast to the Silva Reservoir petition, which, under Article 13 of the side agreement, urged the CEC to report on an environmental problem, the subsequent petitions were Article 14 challenges charging the U.S. government with failing to enforce its own environmental laws.

The ESA challenge was filed in July 1995 by Jay Tutchton of the University of Denver's Earthlaw Center on behalf of five environmental groups: the Biodiversity Legal Foundation, Consejo Asesor Sierra Madre [Sierra Madre Advisory Council], Forest Guardians, Greater Gila Biodiversity Project and the Southwest Center for Biological Diversity. The ESA petition responds to an amendment that Senator Kay Bailey Hutchison (R-TX), attached to a defense appropriations bill signed into law by Clinton in April 1995. The Hutchison amendment rescinds $1.5 million that had been earmarked to make ESA determinations about whether the government should designate a habitat as "critical" or a species as "threatened" or "endangered."

The petition to the CEC argues that the Hutchison Amendment, without repealing or modifying the ESA, effectively halted the habitat and species-listing process, depriving federal agencies of the ability to protect endangered species and enforce important ESA provisions. The environmental group petitioners argued that this amounted to an Article 14 failure of the United States to enforce U.S. environmental law.

The Secretariat's September 1995 decision in the ESA case notes that "the submission impels the Secretariat to consider whether a 'failure to enforce' under Article 14 may result from the enactment of a law which suspends the implementation of certain provisions of another statute." In rejecting the ESA petition, the Secretariat interpreted Article 14 as being limited to "administrative breakdowns (failures) resulting from acts of omissions of an agency or official charged with implementing environmental laws." The Secretariat concluded that, although Article 14 is ambiguous on this point, it was nonetheless intended to be limited to administrative or regulatory failures to enforce environmental laws and not to encompass legislative actions such as the Hutchison Amendment.

"I think it's a narrow reading of the agreement," says Texas Center for Policy Studies' Mary Kelly, who heads the U.S. National Public Advisory Committee, a group of representatives of business, government officials, academics and non-governmental organizations that advises Environmental Protection Agency Administrator Carol Browner in her role as member of the CEC's governing Council.

Tutchton says politics may help explain why the Secretariat did not tackle the ESA petition. "Some of the environmental groups that supported NAFTA criticized us when we filed our petition," he says. "We filed the thing within a week or so of the Congress looking at the [Environmental Protection Agency's] budget in which the contributions to the Secretariat were a line item," he says. "There may have been some desire at the Secretariat not to do anything against the U.S. Congress, which could zero out their funding."

Stressing that he is speaking as an individual, not as the outgoing chair of the CEC's Joint Public Advisory Committee, which is made up of business, government and non-governmental representatives from the three NAFTA countries, Canadian Jacques Gerin acknowledges that the CEC does not exist in a political vacuum. "I went through the reasoning that the [ESA] petitioners put forth and it's good reasoning, it's sustainable," he says. "But I'm not sure you could say to the U.S. Congress that they were *ultra vires* [beyond their legal authority]. I don't think that would have gotten us very far."

A related political factor, Tutchton says, is that some conservative members of Congress are concerned about the loss of U.S. sovereignty under trade agreements, and the ESA petition was filed at a time when NAFTA proponents were seeking fast-track negotiating authority to expand NAFTA to Chile. "I think the Secretariat is trying to thwart this sovereignty argument by sort of writing a check to Congress to say, 'Amend the law in any way you see fit'," Tutchton says.

U.S. Environmental Laxity II: Rampant Logging

Another CEC petition, filed by the Sierra Club Legal Defense Fund (SCLDF) in August 1995 on behalf of 26 environmental groups from all three NAFTA countries, also argues an Article 14 failure to enforce U.S. environmental law. In this case, Seattle-based SCLDF lawyer Patti Goldman contends that a logging rider attached to a disaster assistance appropriations bill, which became law in July 1995, suspends enforcement of U.S. environmental laws for two important programs that govern logging on public lands. The first program is the so-called salvage logging program, which permits harvests of dead and diseased timber. Environmentalists have widely criticized U.S. Forest Service salvage programs, claiming that they are used as an excuse to open up the most ecologically and economically valuable old-growth forest stands to logging. The second is the Option 9 plan, which seeks to balance timber industry interests in logging old-growth forests with the interests of the species that depend on this ecosystem, such as salmon and the spotted owl.

The logging rider provides that any procedures followed by federal agencies for timber sales under these programs automatically satisfy the requirements of federal environmental and natural resource laws—irrespective of how minimal or inadequate these procedures may be. This automatic authorization of timber sales trumps important provisions of the Clean Water Act, the ESA, the National Forest Management Act and the National Environmental Policy Act. In passing such sweeping legislation as a rider to a popular budget-cutting and disaster-assistance bill, Goldman argued that Congress sidestepped the normal legislative process, which provides for public input and congressional hearings. Citizens are also shut out, she contends, by the fact that the rider rules out many of the usual administrative and judicial recourses to challenge violations of environmental law.

Since there were similarities between the ESA and timber petitions, Goldman made a supplementary submission in October 1995, challenging the logic of the Secretariat's rejection of the ESA decision. "By drawing a bright line between legislative enactments and administrative enforcement shortcomings, the Secretariat treats legislative enactments as one homogeneous set of actions," Goldman's brief says. Goldman reasoned that a legislative enactment that defends enforcement activities or prohibits prosecution of a pending enforcement action is little different than an administrative agency's failure to enforce an environmental law, a failure which is clearly in the side agreement's scope. Citing effects of the logging rider that would appear to cut to the heart of the CEC's mission, Goldman wrote that the rider has already allowed timber sales that "experts have concluded may jeopardize the survival of imperiled aquatic species."

The Secretariat's December 8, 1995 logging petition decision acknowledges that some of the failures to enforce environmental laws alleged in the petition "clearly meet the [side agreement's] definitional requirements." Returning to the rationale of its ESA decision, however, the Secretariat argued that "the enactment of legislation which specifically alters the operation of pre-existing environmental law in essence becomes part of the greater body of laws and statutes on the books. This is true even if pre-existing law is not amended or rescinded."

With environmental groups already fuming that the Secretariat drew an unrealistically bright line between legislative and executive administrative functions for a U.S. case, questions are being raised about how much more blurred the lines are in Mexico, where power is highly concentrated in the executive branch and where the executive and other branches have been tightly controlled by one party for almost 70 years.

"If NAFTA means anything about obligations to enforce substantive standards it would go exactly to this point of failure to enforce, regardless of which branch of government is orchestrating the failure," says Michael McCloskey, chair of the Sierra Club and a member of the U.S. National Public Advisory Committee. "If you had a unitary government, a government such as that of Mexico, it would decide it was not going to enforce and that's the end of the story. You don't go into deciding who failed to do it—the government failed to do it."

Babies Without Brains

In Brownsville, Texas and its Mexican sister city across the border, Matamoros, there has been an outbreak of a rare genetic disorder called anencephaly—babies born without brains—an always fatal disease.

The open sewers of Matamoros carry toxic wastes and human refuse. Its factories spew fumes and leak chemicals. Investigators are theorizing that exposure to some toxic chemical kept local mothers from having sufficient folic acid in the crucial first weeks of pregnancy.

The area "is dominated by U.S.-owned companies that came south during the past three decades for cheaper labor, favorable trade rules and lax enforcement of environmental laws."

[*San Francisco Chronicle*, January 8, 1992]

15

Look What the GATT Dragged In

Jean Anne Casey and Colleen Hobbs

The rural town of Hennessey, Oklahoma has just 1,800 people but it is home to the largest hog-breeding company in the world, the British-owned Pig Improvement Company. For urbanites who think that hogs smell like frying bacon and associate pigs with Wilbur in "Charlotte's Web," here's some news: Pork is political, and pigs are an environmental hazard.

Many European companies, hampered from expanding at home by tough pollution laws, are taking advantage of America's less stringent standards. And the General Agreement on Tariffs and Trade will dramatically increase the amount of pork the U.S. can export to Europe: 624,000 metric tons in 1999, up from less than 100,100 tons in 1991. This will make the U.S. the center of global pork production, and companies are rushing to raise hogs in new places. One Danish company even plans to raise 600,000 hogs in Alaska.

The problem with huge hog farms is the manure they produce. The Environmental Protection Agency (EPA) rates animal wastes among the nation's top 10 sources of pollution. Leon Chesnin, a retired University of Nebraska waste management specialist, estimates that the waste generated by 10,000 pigs equals that produced by a city of 17,000 people. If the Pig Improvement Company brings 100,000 hogs to Hennessy, as it plans, the result will be the sewage equivalent of 170,000 people.

"These operations are not family farms," says Barbara Grabner of Prairie Fire Rural Action, a support group for family farms. "They are large corporate ventures that attempt to influence state legislatures to eliminate environmental, corporate farming and zoning laws." The result, she says, is "environmental classism" that exploits the residents of sparsely populated areas.

Corporate hog farms collect feces and urine into small ponds lined with plastic sheeting, called lagoons, and the wastes are later used as fertilizer. In practice, this system allows nitrates to leach into the water table and enter the drinking supply. Nitrate contamination can result in circulatory problems, and in extreme cases has caused a condition called blue baby syndrome that can be fatal to infants. Pig waste also gives off air-borne ammonia, which can cause respiratory ailments.

How bad can the contamination get? Bob Bergland, the Secretary of Agriculture under President Jimmy Carter, said in March 1994 that the super-concentrated pig industry in North Carolina was in danger of "collapse" because in some counties the "ground is saturated with hog manure."

The huge livestock companies say that they are just honest farmers and that standard E.P.A. regulations keep them from making much of a profit. Don't believe it. These are nothing less than factories, and their proliferation is an indication of their profitability. Like any other manufacturing industry, state and Federal regulators should institute and enforce strict controls on emissions.

16

Shrugging Off an Attack on the Clean Air Act

Norman Solomon

The news should have caused a national uproar: In early 1996, a global trade authority ordered the United States to allow higher levels of air pollution or pay huge fines. But, if you blinked, you may have missed the story entirely.

In a decision with momentous implications, the new World Trade Organization ruled that the U.S. law known as the Clean Air Act is unacceptable because of restrictions it places on pollutants in imported gasoline. The decree could result in higher levels of toxic auto emissions.

"This is a major blow to the ability of the United States to protect public health," said a senior attorney for the Natural Resources Defense Council.

But when the news broke in mid-January 1996, it was a fleeting blip on the media screen. Since then, follow-up coverage has been almost impossible to find.

Why did such a dramatic—and important—story drop from sight so quickly? Because none of this nation's top movers and shakers wanted to make a big deal out of it.

The White House preferred that the story disappear, pronto. After all, the World Trade Organization owes its existence to the GATT trade pact that President Clinton pushed through Congress in late 1994.

Back then, Clinton vowed that the accord would not interfere with U.S. anti-pollution laws. His trade representative, Mickey Kantor, even claimed that the GATT agreement "will help improve environmental protection."

Yet, in the wake of the WTO's outrageous ruling January 17, 1996, leading Republicans were not well-positioned to turn it into a campaign issue. Sen. Bob Dole has lamented the enormous power of the WTO, but there's no escaping the reality that he voted to create it in the first place. On Capitol Hill, most Democrats—eager to cover for Clinton—remained silent about the WTO's action.

Stymied by public opinion that has forced congressional Republicans to back off from efforts to gut laws like the Clean Air Act, many corporate polluters now view the World Trade Organization as a godsend.

Multinational oil companies are quietly savoring the WTO's decision. They see big dollar signs ahead, with surging U.S. imports of dirty gasoline from outmoded foreign refineries.

What about environmental organizations? The sad truth is that the largest ones have gotten into the habit of muting their voices in deference to the White House.

One of the most independent advocacy groups—Public Citizen, founded by Ralph Nader—has not minced words. "Under the WTO, countries and their democratically elected representatives are very limited in what they can do to implement and enforce environmental objectives," says Lori Wallach, director of the group's Global Trade Watch. Because of the WTO ruling on gasoline, Wallach told me, the United States must make "an unacceptable choice between allowing more polluted air or facing enormous sanctions—$150 million a year."

Welcome to global "free trade," WTO style.

[*Editor's Note*: On June 19, 1996 the Clinton administration agreed to honor the WTO ruling by promising to change the way the U.S. government applies environmental regulations to imported gasoline.]

Section 4

Resistance and Alternatives

Although our analysis thus far has focused on the planet-threatening power of corporations, there *is* reason for hope. The transnational alliance of elites is strong, but so is the growing anti-systemic movement for fundamental change. There is an alternative form of globalization being built up from the grassroots community level. This work is being done by ordinary citizens who are committed to creating a world in which human community and environmental sustainability replace greed and profit-seeking as the dominant values.

In the first chapter of this section, "Global Reach: Workers Fight the Multinationals," John Cavanagh and Robin Broad examine the "internationalist anti-corporate stance" that is gaining more converts every day to a new kind of politics that links the interests of working people in wealthy countries such as the United States with the interests of workers in Third World countries. In his essay "A Common Sense Citizens' Agenda," David Korten lays out a detailed list of reforms that could be made in the global political-economic order to facilitate real democracy and raise living standards for the majority. In "Don't Waste Time with Politicians—Organize!" Baldemar Velasquez explains the successful strategy used by the Farm Labor Organizing Committee (FLOC) in building grassroots links with Mexican workers and forcing large corporations to accept union demands for better wages and working conditions. In "The U.S.-Salvador Gap," Gayle Liles traces the political struggle that produced an historic agreement by which The Gap clothing store chain agreed to allow independent monitoring of the factories it buys clothing from in El Salvador. In his essay "A Better Way to Measure the Economy," Ted Halstead of Redefining Progress explains the absurdity of measuring economic activity with Gross National Product and he proposes a replacement: the Genuine Progress Indicator which incorporates environmental and social costs, and generally gives a more accurate measure of the way the economy works in real life. Steven Hill then takes us to Pennsylvania in "Stakeholders vs. Stockholders" to examine how that state created legislation that protected local jobs and strengthened the principle that "stakeholders" (workers, consumers, local communities) have a legitimate interest in corporate decision-making that should be considered along with the interest of stockholders. In "The New Protectionism," Colin Hines and Tim Lang rehabilitate the verb 'protect' and lay out a grand strategy showing how nations and local economies could be protected from the ravages of globalization without necessarily touching off the trade wars that some believe were a key part of the Great Depression of the 1930s.

The book concludes with a summary of the key areas needing reform and ways for you to contact the groups who are leading the charge.

17

Global Reach:
Workers Fight the Multinationals

John Cavanagh and Robin Broad

At various times over the years, politicians have tried to gain political mileage from the debate over free trade versus protectionism. Yet the debate is gradually breaking out of these narrow confines thanks to the movement to attach labor and environmental conditions to trade agreements and hundreds of efforts to press corporations to abide by codes of conduct.

Consider the Nike story. Over the past two decades, Nike closed its New Hampshire and Maine factories and increasingly subcontracted work to factories it did not own in Korea and Taiwan, where workers were poorly paid and denied basic rights. As unions spread in both of those countries, Nike shifted its suppliers primarily to Indonesia, China and Thailand, where they could depend on governments to suppress independent union-organizing efforts.

In 1992 Nike paid part-time employee Michael Jordan some $20 million: more than the combined yearly income of the thousands of young women who toiled under horrendous conditions to piece together Nike sneakers for suppliers in Indonesia. The year before, a reporter had asked Nike's general manager there about employers hitting workers and other labor abuses in these factories. The manager replied, "It's not within our scope to investigate." He did say he was aware "of labor disturbances in the six factories that make Nike shoes," but he did not know what they were about. "I don't know that I need to know."

Today, after numerous exposés and creative pressure by labor, religious and other activist groups across North America and Europe, Nike acknowledges that working conditions in the factories that it contracts with overseas are its own responsibility. It has passed its own internal code of conduct to establish labor guidelines for its suppliers, as has its competitor Reebok.

There is still a long way to go, labor rights advocates remind us. In particular, they are pressing Nike and other companies to agree to two more steps. First, Nike's code does not demand that its suppliers respect workers' rights to form unions and bargain collectively—key elements in the fight for livable wages and benefits. Second, Nike has yet to agree to spot-checks in factories by independent monitors to insure compliance.

Meanwhile, labor rights activists for the International Labor Rights Fund in Washington, D.C., moved to pressure companies on another front. In 1992 they filed a petition before the U.S. government's trade office charging that Indonesia allows systematic violation of workers' rights, and hence should be denied special trade privileges under a 1984 law that conditions the privileges on countries' respect for these rights. The Indonesian government responded to the pressure by announcing a 29 percent raise in the minimum wage in 1994, so Nike and other manufacturers have been forced to raise wages. Similar, albeit weaker, labor (and environmental) language attached to NAFTA allows citizens to challenge corporate violations of national law before a tri-national commission.

Twenty years ago, Institute for Policy Studies co-founder Richard Barnet, along with Ronald Muller, asked (in their book *Global Reach*) which forces could become a "countervailing power" against global corporations. Barnet focused on the strength of labor unions in the middle third of the twentieth century and the promise of more aggressive government action at local and national levels.

Today, governments are more compromised than ever in succumbing to corporate demands, and trade-union movements around the world have weakened. Yet countervailing power is emerging, and it appears strongest when it derives from new coalitions of movements coordinating across labor, environmental, consumer and other social sectors and across geographical borders.

Take the dramatic victory in a campaign organized against the clothing store The Gap by the National Labor Committee, the textile union UNITE, religious groups and allies in Central America. The National Labor Committee had generated widespread publicity around the dismal working conditions of girls as young as 13, who toil in Central American sweatshops up to seventy hours a week earning less than 60 cents an hour. The committee brought two such workers who sew clothes for The Gap and other U.S. companies on a tour through the United States. As religious and other activists joined the chorus of disapproval, The Gap announced it would leave El Salvador and shift to suppliers in other countries. Then activists broadened the campaign, demanding that The Gap stay in El Salvador, pressure its contractors to respect basic worker rights and allow independent monitoring of a Gap code of conduct. On December 15, 1995, in the midst of the Christmas shopping season, The Gap agreed to these demands.

Part of the success of the Gap campaign was the growing understanding by U.S. workers that their own interests now lie in helping workers elsewhere. As long as there are sweatshops in El Salvador, U.S. companies will use the cheaper labor there to bargain down wages and working conditions in this country. In January 1996, UNITE joined with the National Consumers League and other groups to launch a movement against sweatshops at home and abroad. Consumers also seem willing to use their purchasing power to help workers. More than three-fourths of consumers polled in a 1995 Marymount University survey of more than 1,000 adults said that they would avoid purchasing goods made in sweatshops, even if they had to pay a higher price.

Success in these campaigns requires both concerted citizen pressure and strong links between activists at home and abroad.

In May 1995, religious, labor, consumer and other U.S. groups that make up the Child Labor Coalition launched a consumer boycott of Bangladeshi clothing exports after investigations revealed widespread child labor in the industry. The threat of a boycott convinced the Bangladesh Garment Manufacturers and Exporters Association to sign an agreement with UNICEF and the International Labor Organization to move some 25,000 children out of the clothing industry and into schools.

Close to $1 million from the three parties to the agreement will go toward verifying the end of child labor, schooling for the former child workers and a modest stipend to the families of the children. One of the most novel features of the agreement is that the Bangladeshi garment companies agreed to let the I.L.O. train independent monitors to carry out spot-checks on clothing factories. As with all such agreements, constant vigilance will be necessary to insure compliance.

Similar campaigns are forcing other companies to act, particularly in the clothing, footwear and toy industries, where corporations have shifted a great deal of production overseas. Even the rapidly expanding coffee-bar chains have proved to be targets. The threat of a consumer boycott prompted Starbucks in October 1995 to release a "Framework for a Code of Conduct" in which it pledged to improve working conditions at coffee suppliers in Guatemala and elsewhere.

Such campaigns work best against companies that depend on strong consumer brand loyalty, like Nike and Starbucks, and less well in industries in which there isn't strong brand awareness (paper-clip manufacturers), or where the consumers are other companies (auto parts). Likewise, campaigns that focus on child labor, sweatshops or the environment appeal to more U.S. consumers than campaigns to respect union rights. Success will also depend upon developing a monitoring capacity in country after country to hold companies to their promises.

Nor do corporate targets sit by idly in the face of attacks. It cost only pocket change for mining powerhouse Freeport McMoRan to purchase a two-page advertisement in *The New*

York Times to counter an environmentalist campaign against the devastating impact of the company's Indonesian mines on indigenous communities and the environment. And the fact that most major media outlets are controlled by large corporations makes it more difficult to get any story, let alone a positive one, about citizen campaigns on corporations into the mainstream media.

Although it is a position that will not get much play from the mainstream media, a third way is emerging between the extremes of free trade and nationalistic protectionism. This third way includes three often overlapping tendencies. At one end of the spectrum are the radical environmentalists and localization advocates, with their campaigns to kick Kentucky Fried Chicken out of India, spare small-town America from Wal Mart and prevent pharmaceutical firms from patenting products derived from trees and other life forms. Another stream includes Ralph Nader and many of the anti-NAFTA and anti-World Trade Organization coalitions, who have tried to slow down globalization by defeating trade agreements.

Finally, other citizen movements are seeking to reshape globalization by rendering it more "socially and environmentally responsible." This includes the above-mentioned drives to add enforceable labor and environmental standards to trade agreements and the pressure on Starbucks and other companies for tough corporate codes. There is also a growing alternative trading movement that bypasses large corporate channels to deliver products made under more humane and sustainable conditions from cooperatives directly to consumers.

Despite some tensions, these various strains of a third way came dramatically together in North America in the grassroots, national and cross-border alliances that fought against NAFTA. Since the NAFTA fight, these forces have linked with other citizen movements in Europe and parts of the Third World in arenas such as the International Forum on Globalization. This group, headquartered in San Francisco but with participants from nineteen countries, organized a teach-in on globalization in New York's Riverside Church in November that drew 1,800 people.

Similar strands came together that same weekend in Japan when more than 120 Asian citizen groups met to protest plans for a NAFTA-style free-trade area in Asia.

Part of what unites these forces is an internationalist anti-corporate stance that counters the nationalistic populism of far right ideologues such as Patrick Buchanan. Canadian anti-NAFTA leader Tony Clarke is heading an effort in several countries to pull together activists around the theme of "challenging corporate rule," by which he means challenging not only abuse of workers and the environment by corporations but also their growing grip on political agendas all over the world.

The success of these efforts will depend in large part on moving beyond labor, environmental and religious alliances to harness and organize consumer power. The United States still accounts for a quarter of the measured economic activity on the planet. Hence U.S. consumers hold the power to demand significant changes in the way goods are produced. There is as yet, however, little experience in the kind of massive consumer-labor-environmental-community coalitions that will be required for success. The future of popular efforts to transform trade and investment in a global economy will depend on innovations in organizing that break down traditional barriers among constituencies and across borders.

18

A Common Sense Citizens' Agenda

David Korten

It hasn't been easy to create an economic system able to produce 358 billionaires while keeping another 1.3 billion people living in absolute deprivation. It took long and dedicated effort by legions of economists, lawyers, and politicians on the payrolls of monied interests to design and implement such a system. It required a radical altering of the dominant culture and the restructuring of many important institutions. It will take a similarly committed effort on the part of civil society to design and put in place an economic system supportive of economic justice and environmental sustainability.

To reclaim our economic spaces, we must first reclaim our political spaces from the corporations and other big money interests that control them. This will require far more than incremental or marginal changes. The following are among the measures probably required.

• *Prohibit political advertising on television.* TV political ads are far more often misleading than informative; they are extremely expensive; they discredit the political system and give inordinate power in deciding elections to those with big money. Instead, electronic communications media that enjoy access to the public airways should be required as part of their public service obligation to provide ample time for debates, interviews, and roundtables with political candidates—thus giving the public in-depth exposure to their ideas and personalities.

• *Place strict limits on individual campaign contributions.* The principle of democracy is one person one vote, not one dollar one vote.

• *Place strict limits on campaign spending.* We want to know what a political candidate can do with a limited budget, not how effectively he or she can manipulate us with large amounts of money.

• *Strip corporations of their fictitious rights of an individual.* Take appropriate legislative action to put aside the legal fabrication that corporations have the same rights as individuals. Only living things have natural rights.

• *Get corporations entirely out of politics.* Corporations are public bodies created by public charter to serve a public purpose. It is the responsibility of the corporation to obey the rules that people choose to set for them, not *make* the rules. Therefore, corporations should be barred from making political contributions of any kind. Indeed, they should also be barred from any involvement in politics and political advocacy—including the solicitation of their employees, shareholders, sales outlets, and suppliers to make either political contributions or representations on political or public policy matters. Corporate charitable contributions should also be prohibited in recognition of their widespread abuse to advance corporate political aims. The corporation's workers and individual shareholders—not corporate management—should make their own decisions as to how their shares of corporate income will be allocated for political and charitable purposes.

• *Eliminate the concentration of media ownership.* To avoid concentration of media power and assure a diversity of political voices, the communications media should be subjected to strict anti-trust provisions prohibiting any single individual or corporation from owning more than one major electronic or print media outlet. This would both increase the diversity of independent editorial voices and strengthen competition in the media industry.

• *Take back the corporate charter.* Facilitate citizen action to withdraw the charters of corporations that demonstrate disregard for the law or otherwise fail to serve the public good.

Reclaiming Our Economic Spaces

One of the fundamental points on which Adam Smith and Karl Marx agreed is that workers should own their means of production. Though not widely noted, in the small enterprises of Adam Smith's ideal economy the worker was generally also the owner and manager. Furthermore, Smith assumed that enterprises would be locally owned and that their owners would thus be imbedded in a framework of local community values and interests. While Smith believed in the benefits of trade, he considered it logical that most markets would be local because of the costs and uncertainties of trading with foreign lands. He took an especially dim view of large corporations with absentee owners that used their political and market power to extract monopoly profits.

Our present globalized economic system affirms much of the wisdom of Smith's vision. The more economic power becomes highly concentrated and detached from any local interest, the more surely it is used to benefit the power holders at the expense of larger community interests.

If we intend that markets allocate resources efficiently in the public interest, then we must restructure them to fulfill the appropriate conditions—much as Smith defined them. Thus, it will be necessary to break up large concentrations of economic power, re-establish the connection between investment returns and productive activity, create incentives for producers to internalize their costs, and root the ownership of capital locally in people and communities engaged primarily in local production to meet local needs. It will also be necessary to reduce and slow international financial flows, deflate the global pool of extractive capital, and favor long-term over short-term investment.

The needed restructuring is appropriately guided by a vision of a global system of localized economies that reduce the scale of economic activity and link economic decisions to their consequences. Working out the details of an appropriate policy agenda will require our best minds and substantial experimentation. The following are some of the measures that should be considered.

• A 0.5 percent financial transactions tax on the purchase and sale of financial instruments such as stocks, bonds, foreign currencies, and derivatives to discourage short-term speculation and arbitraging.

• A graduated surtax on short-term capital gains to make most speculation unprofitable, stabilize financial markets, and lengthen investment perspectives without penalizing long-term productive investment. The surtax on the sale of an asset held less than a week might be as high as 80 percent.

• A 100 percent reserve requirement on demand deposits to reduce the ability of the financial system to create money by pyramiding loans. This would make it possible to restore the connection between the creation of money and the creation of wealth.

• Preferential treatment of community banks. Governments should guarantee only deposits placed in unitary community banks that channel most of their funds back to the community.

• Rigorous enforcement of anti-trust laws to break up concentrations of corporate power. Buy-out and merger proposals should be subject to intensive and skeptical governmental review with the burden of proof resting on the proposing party to show that the proposal will advance the long-term public—not just short-term investor—interests.

• Worker and community buy-outs. Before a major corporation is allowed to close a plant or undertake a sale or merger, the affected workers and community should have a legal right of first option to buy out the assets on preferential terms. The terms should reflect the workers' years of personal investment of their labor in the company and the collective investment of the local community in public facilities that have made the company's local operations possible. Bankruptcy rules should be structured similarly to give employees and communities a buy-out option. Similarly, when a company is required to divest parts of its operation under antitrust, employees and/or the community should have first option to buy the divested units. Government oversight should assure that such buy-outs are structured so that workers and/or communities have real control. Rules governing company pension funds might be revised to allow their use by employees to purchase voting control of their firm's assets.

• Tax Shifting. Corporate tax law should be revised to shift taxes from things that benefit society (such as employment, employer contributions to social security, health care and workman's compensation) toward taxing activities that contribute to social and environmental dysfunction (such as resource extraction, packaging, pollution, energy use, imports, corporate lobbying and advertising).

• Annual Profit Payout. Corporate income taxes should be eliminated simultaneously with the introduction of a requirement that corporations pay out their profits each year to their shareholders. These profits would thus be taxed as shareholder income at the shareholder's normal marginal rate. Corporations would then have no incentive to shift profits around the world to the jurisdiction with the lowest tax rate. Interest payments on debt financing would come directly out of profits, rather than out of taxes, thus discouraging the use of debt financing and making most corporate buyouts unprofitable.

• Corporate Subsidies. Welfare reform should give top priority to getting dependent corporations off the welfare rolls.

• Intellectual Property. The appropriate purpose of intellectual property rights protection is to provide incentives for research and creative contribution, not to create protected information monopolies. Intellectual property rights should be defined and interpreted narrowly and granted only for the minimum period of time necessary to allow those who invest in research to recover their costs and a reasonable profit. The patenting of any life form or genetic process, any discovery funded with public moneys, or any process or technology that gives the holder effective monopoly control over a type of research or class of products should be precluded by law.

• Advertising. Those forms of advertising that serve to encourage consumption rather than simply inform prospective customers regarding the availability and specifications of products should be banned. This will at once eliminate an important market advantage of large corporations and remove an important underpinning of the consumer culture.

Economic Equity and Security

Inequality makes it possible for those with economic power to pass the costs of their unsustainable consumption onto the economically weak and encourages extravagant consumption by the few. Economic insecurity creates a significant incentive for individuals to accumulate wealth beyond their real need. Public policies that favor economic equality and assure basic economic security should move us toward sustainability as well. Appropriate measures may include:

• A guaranteed income sufficient to meet basic needs;

• Highly progressive income and consumption taxes on levels of income and consumption above those required to comfortably meet basic needs;

• Taxation of inheritance and trust income at the same rate as any other income to avoid creating a perpetual privileged class and to provide an incentive for the offspring of wealthy families to make their own creative contribution; and

• A reduced workweek to allocate available employment equitably.

International Reforms

A number of reforms are required at the global level to remove important sources of injustice and restrain the power of transnational capital. These include:

• Eliminating international debts of low income countries. The public international debts of low income countries should be eliminated through a two step process. Odious debts contracted without public consent or for purposes that did not serve public purposes should be repudiated through appropriate internationally sanctioned legal processes to pass the costs onto the responsible individuals and financial institutions. The remaining debts should be repaid out of an international fund under agreements that preclude recreating them.

• Closing the World Bank as part of the plan to end the process of international debt creation. It is time to recognize that creating an institution to increase the debts of poor countries was simply a bad idea.

• Placing an international financial transactions tax on all spot transactions in foreign exchange to dampen speculative currency movements. The funds generated should be used to retire Third World debt and fund the United Nations.

• Closing the World Trade Organization (WTO) and the International Monetary Fund (IMF) and transferring responsibility for international economic management to the United Nations, with the mandate to maintain a balanced and equitable system of economic relationships among nations that encourages and supports substantial environmental and economic self-reliance. Responsibilities would include negotiating and enforcing agreements establishing standards of conduct for transnational corporations, coordinating international antitrust action, and protecting the rights of all nations to choose with whom they will trade, under what terms, and to set rules and standards for businesses operating in their jurisdictions. Decision-making processes should be transparent and open to public participation.

• Monitor cross border environmental flows. Establish an international monitoring system to report imbalances in flows of environmental resources between countries as a step toward limiting the ability of one country to pass the environmental burdens of its consumption to another.

This is an admittedly full agenda. And it is surely incomplete. There is no simple fix for a system as badly broken as the one we presently have. This list is illustrative of the types of measures that must be considered. There is need for a vigorous public debate toward building a broadly based political consensus in support of comprehensive citizen agendas for national and international reforms adequate to the task of building just and sustainable societies for the new millennium.

> *"I hope we shall crush in its birth the aristocracy of our moneyed corporations, which dare already to challenge our government to a trial of strength and bid defiance to the laws of our country."*
>
> Thomas Jefferson

19

Don't Waste Time With Politicians — Organize!

Baldemar Velasquez

We at the Farm Labor Organizing Committee (FLOC) believe that we must treat the internationalization of the economy as an organizing issue, not a legislative one. America's electoral politics are woefully inadequate to address the broad international issues facing workers around the world. FLOC considers political and legislative maneuvering to be a dead-end response for labor in this country. Why attempt to negotiate with politicians? Why not organize the industries run by the multinational corporations, and negotiate directly with the people who are going to make a difference?

Some labor activists focus their attention on free trade agreements. However, in the case of NAFTA, we got very few actual labor protections written into the agreement, and predictably, they aren't being enforced any better than existing labor laws. In general, legislation may involve important philosophical concepts, but it will not make a difference in favor of working people in this country. The NAFTA accord cannot protect workers' interest in side-bar agreements because neither the United States nor Mexico has the political will and apparatus to effectively enforce worker rights under existing legislation.

Instead of funding politicians, our unions ought to fund and help organize community groups around the world that will be part of the future organizing environment. The internationalization of the trade union movement is now an absolute necessity. Negotiating and cooperating in these struggles with other unions and organizations threatened by the same corporations and forces in power is the only way we're going to gain better conditions. We all know that organizing workers is what gives us political control because of the direct economic pressure we can bring to bear. Then, out of that organizing will come laws that we hope will institutionalize what has already been built by the unions through organization. An organizer can't depend on trying to go about it the other way, with legislation guiding the way.

This approach to organizing is very hard work and usually doesn't pay off right away. In many ways, we organizers have to think of the new challenges before us in the global economy as a time of analysis and rebuilding our unions. It's essential to understand that the actions needed right now are simply not going to make our unions any bigger or even stronger at first. But FLOC's experiences with U.S. and Mexican workers have demonstrated how organizing provides empowerment, contracts, and, in our minds, is the only way for unions to really win in today's global situation.

Campbell's Victory Sets Stage for International Organizing

FLOC's breakthrough in the Midwest set some important precedents for organizing without collective bargaining laws, and challenging the archaic structure of sharecropping. After an initial strike of over 2,600 workers in 1978, FLOC continued strikes, a boycott and a corporate campaign against Campbell Soup for eight years. Arrests, beatings, violent attacks, a cross burning from the Ku Klux Klan, and intense harassment from the sheriff's department were resisted with nonviolent sit-in demonstrations, marches and strikes. The central issue in this fight was Campbell's refusal to bargain with our membership because they were not Campbell employees. Indeed they were not, as they worked on their contracted supplier farms. Twenty independent family farms grew their supply of tomatoes where our people were employed. In 1986, a miraculous breakthrough occurred when Campbell

signed a contract with FLOC and a hastily assembled association representing the 20 tomato growers.

This was the first multi-party collective bargaining agreement
in labor history. Part of the negotiations process included the
establishment of an independent commission, chaired by former
Labor Secretary John Dunlop, to oversee representation procedures and collective negotiations.

One piece of Campbell's bargaining strategy was a threat to
import more tomato paste from their suppliers in Mexico.
Campbell was resistant to raising wages from $3.35 (then the
minimum wage) to $4.50. Out-sourcing from Mexico represented
an attempt by Campbell to apply external pressure as we approached negotiations. In 1987-88, FLOC began to develop a
relationship with Mexico's Campbell workers. Our message to
Mexico's unions was simple: we told them that we wanted to
help get the best agreement we could, because the better it was,
the better negotiating position we would be in. After a number of
cross-border visits, a large church symposium in Mexico, and a
demonstration at Campbell's Sinaloa tomato paste factory, the
Mexican union won its best contract ever. Subsequently, in our
negotiations with Campbell in 1989, not one word was spoken
about cheaper tomatoes from Mexico.

FLOC's Latest International Campaign

Today, we face a similar situation with Ohio and Michigan's
major pickle and cucumber companies. Vlasic and Dean Foods
do the same type of contracting with small family farmers for
pickles as Campbell does with tomatoes. They also contract pickles in North Carolina and the Mexican states of Michoacan and
Guanajuato. Organization of their contracted farms was more
daunting because of the larger number of farms (about 90 farms)
and more than 5,000 workers split into units of 30 to 60 workers.
Additionally, these sharecropping workers were technically independent contractors with no protection under the U.S. Farm
Labor Standards Act, workers compensation or unemployment
compensation. They were also taxed the full 17 percent self-

employed Social Security Tax.

Using the multi-party tomato agreement as a precedent, we were able to organize that mess relatively quickly: Heinz USA and Vlassic in 1987-88; and Dean Foods subsidiaries, Aunt Jane Pickles and Green Bay Foods in 1992. Three separate growers' associations were set up to accommodate these multi-party agreements. Sharecropping was wiped out from the entire pickle industry in a single orchestrated step in 1993. These workers now enjoy employee status for the first time.

Now that structural changes have been achieved, we have begun to negotiate for standard benefits in our contracts. As we increase wages, the pressure begins from the cheaper sources in North Carolina and Mexico, where some acreage has already shifted. As part of our Mexico work, we negotiated an agreement with Mexico's largest farmworker union, calling for the establishment of a U.S.-Mexico commission to oversee joint organizing, negotiations and other forms of collaboration among common workforces for the same multinational corporations.

In the midst of the intense political warfare that rages throughout Mexico, this commission is helping us connect and establish relationships for action with the common worker. This effort brought home to FLOC the realization that what we were attempting to do was build a borderless community of workers.

If we succeed, it is possible to see a breakthrough in signing an international agreement that would cover a corporation's workers in more than one country. As we move toward this goal in the pickle industry, FLOC has finished the protocol work with Mexico's unions in their related production areas. Only when we organize workers and communities, wherever a particular corporation does business, will we be in a position to stop companies from pitting us against each other. Organizing an entire industry is not a radical idea, it's just that we have to do it internationally. This will turn the downward spiral of competition into an upward spiral of worker collaboration.

FLOC's U.S.-Mexico Exchange Program has been used as a model for future unionism because of its successful communication, joint action, and development of leadership across borders. For unions that are interested in doing international work with a focus on organizing, here are some practical points:

• Investigate and learn to understand the relationship between local production and the global economy. Don't expect immediate dramatic gains or victories. Take the time to make an analysis of the international industry and lay a new foundation.

• Find out where the workers around the world are located. Arrange to have workers in your area visit them, and get to know their needs and concerns. Develop strong relationships and friendships.

• Establish international agreements of solidarity and collaboration with these workers and their organizations.

• Put in the hard work it takes to organize the whole industry.

• Determine your allies among other groups, including management groups, who can apply pressure on international corporate management, and meet with those allies to establish your common interests and need for cooperative alliance.

• Negotiate directly with the industries that have the money and power to make changes, rather than spending time lobbying politicians.

We believe these organizing steps are critical to challenge the global financiers who are scavenging the earth for speculative opportunities. America's trade union movement can play a key role in reshaping the economic landscape and bringing democracy to corporations which would otherwise have financial and economic hegemony over peoples and communities.

"Insist on Corporate Accountability"

The following is excerpted from Congressional Testimony by Shirley Reinhardt, a 'downsized' General Electric worker.

When I got fired is when my education really began.

... we have learned that the problems are a lot bigger than we thought. The problems are global. In fact, I have come to believe that trade policy and unemployment are all tied up together.

In July of 1991, I went on a trip to Mexico that was sponsored by the Tennessee Industrial Renewal Network (TIRN). The things and people we saw on our trip we will never forget. I guess I thought I had already learned that corporations seem to care first and foremost about their own profits and are willing to treat workers and communities as expendable as long as it is to their own advantage. But nothing I had learned had prepared me to see the conditions under which workers in Mexico are forced to live.

One room houses overflowing with people, suffocating summer heat filling the tiny boxes where mothers fanned their sweating babies, stagnant pools of water with scum and garbage right next to where people were living, drainpipes carrying toxic industrial waste into ditches that ran through neighborhoods, bare feet, sick animals, horrible smells and open sores.

And yet it is a strange thing. These pictures in my mind don't last as long as other pictures: many of the people we met had a courage and dignity I will never forget. Against huge odds they were fighting to build a life. They were beautiful people.

They asked us to bring back the word to you about what is happening to those on the bottom in Mexico, because what is happening ought to be a crime. And it is hurting not only Mexicans, it is a direct threat to the standard of living of American workers.

Our government should insist on corporate accountability. Instead, it rewards irresponsibility. Our government should set ground rules so companies are not pressured to compete with each other on the basis of how much they can gouge their workers. Instead, it pushes a version of free trade that encourages low-wage competition.

20

The U.S.-Salvador Gap

Gayle Liles

Yielding to mounting criticism from consumers, labor organizers and activists over human rights abuses in Central American *maquiladoras*, The Gap has become the first major multinational retailer to agree to independent monitoring of its contractors. On December 15, 1995, representatives from The Gap and the National Labor Committee Education Fund in Support of Worker and Human Rights in Central America (NLC) signed an agreement which granted observers from the Human Rights Ombudsman Office in El Salvador, the Washington, D.C.-based Interfaith Center for Corporate Responsibility (ICCR) and other human rights groups access to the plant of The GAP's Salvadoran contractor, Taiwanese-owned Mandarin International, and laid the foundation for a system of continued third-party monitoring to assure Mandarin's compliance with The Gap's "Guidelines for Vendor Conduct." The Gap stopped placing orders with Mandarin, and agreed to resume them only when Mandarin and the government of El Salvador "demonstrate an ability to effectively investigate and resolve labor disputes fairly, justly, and promptly," and ensure "that our orders will result in humane and productive employment in El Salvador."

"The Gap has now set a new standard for the protection of human rights—especially the rights of women and workers," said Charles Kernaghan, executive director of the New York City-based NLC. "The Gap listened to its consumers and has taken a significant step in accepting direct responsibility for how and under what conditions its products are made."

Kathleen Bertlesen, a spokeswoman for The Gap, emphasized that the agreement applies only "to independent monitoring of the company's contractors in El Salvador." She declined to comment on whether The Gap would permit similar monitoring of its other overseas contractors. According to its 1994 annual report, The Gap purchases 70 percent of its merchandise from overseas vendors in 47 different countries.

With its precedent-setting emphasis on enforcement of codes of conduct for contractors and reliance on third-party monitoring, The GAP-NLC accord could become a model with far-reaching implications. *Maquiladora* (assembly plant) exports have skyrocketed in the last decade, especially in labor-intensive industries like garment making. *Maquiladora* exports from El Salvador to the United States alone rose from $10.2 million in 1985 to $398 million in 1994. The number of Salvadoran *maquiladora* workers producing for the U.S. market increased from 3,500 to 50,000. At the same time, however, real *maquiladora* wages fell 53 percent—to the current 56 cents an hour—which provides just 18.1 percent of the annual basic needs of a family of four.

Although many retailers require their contractors to adhere to a corporate Code of Conduct to ensure that their plants meet minimum health and safety standards—The Gap has had such "sourcing guidelines" in place for several years—they are rarely enforced in practice, and workers are generally ignorant of their rights under these rules. None of the Mandarin workers were aware of The Gap's Code of Conduct, according to Judith Viera, a former Mandarin employee. Even if it had been posted prominently in the factory, it would have done the workers little good; the code had never been translated into Spanish. As part of the agreement reached between The Gap and the NLC, The Gap's Code of Conduct will be translated into Spanish, Korean and Chinese so that both workers and plant managers will understand exactly what The Gap expects of them.

Last summer the NLC conducted a campaign to raise public awareness of the abuses Central American *maquiladora* workers regularly endure. In response to worsening conditions in *maquiladoras* in Honduras, Guatemala, and El Salvador, the NLC took two young *maquiladora* workers on a 20-city tour of the United States and Canada. The women's testimony forced many North American consumers to confront, for the first time, the suffering thousands—primarily young women and girls—bear for fashion's sake. The tour garnered national media attention and prompted public demonstrations and letter-writing campaigns to pressure The Gap into taking responsibility for the enforcement of its own Code of Conduct. "The response was amazing," says Kernaghan. "People were not only furious—they wanted to act."

One of the women, 18-year-old Judith Viera, worked in the Mandarin plant making T-shirts for The Gap. She provided her audiences with a harrowing description of conditions during her tenure at the Mandarin sweatshop. Although the workweek was supposed to be only 44 hours long, at least 8 additional hours of overtime were required and uncompensated. Refusal to work overtime typically resulted in termination the next day. The drinking water in the plant was contaminated, and the air choked with dust. During work hours, talking was strictly forbidden, and loud music was piped into the factory to encourage a relentless pace. Bathroom visits required special passes, and were restricted to two per day.

Viera was among the Mandarin workers who formed the Union of Workers of the Mandarin International Company (SETMI) in February 1995—the first legally recognized union ever formed in a Salvadoran free trade zone—to protest the low wages and inhumane conditions at the sweatshop. Almost immediately afterwards, Mandarin began a coordinated campaign of brutality and terrorism designed to destroy the union.

According to the NLC, Mandarin "hired two dozen ex-military, plain-clothed, armed 'security guards'. The women workers were told their union would have to disappear one way or another, or 'blood will flow'. Since the creation of the union, the plant's 850 workers have endured multiple lock-outs, more than 100 union members have been fired and union sympathizers have been beaten and threatened with termination unless they renounce the union."

In entering the agreement with the NLC, The GAP acknowledges the legitimacy of SETMI and pledges to make Mandarin choose between accepting the union and giving up lucrative Gap contracts. Although SETMI is pleased with the agreement, there is some question about how Mandarin will respond. Kernaghan concedes that "it is still unclear whether Mandarin will reinstate the fired union workers." El Salvador instituted a Labor Code intended to guard against abuses like Mandarin's, but its Ministry of Labor is woefully understaffed and underfunded, and is currently in little position to enforce its own rules.

It will thus be up to workers and their supporters—in El Salvador and around the world—to keep up the pressure on companies like Mandarin. Ron Blackwell, an economist with the Union of Needletrades, Industrial and Textile Employees (UNITE), says, "The only party in industry that has unqualified interest in enforcement are workers, and the only party in industry with unqualified interest in violations are workers." With the workers of the world watching, El Salvador, as Kernaghan puts it, "could become an example and inspiration for all of Central America and the Caribbean."

Democracy and the Market

"As nations move toward equilibrium they ought to be governed by a global economic system that pushes the bottom up rather than pulling the top down ... the democratic imperative is nothing less than that: to refashion the global economy so that it runs uphill for everyone, so that it enhances democracy rather than crippling it, so that the economic returns are distributed widely among all classes instead of narrowly at the top."

From William Greider, "The Global Marketplace: A Closet Dictator," in Ralph Nader, ed., The Case Against Free Trade *(San Francisco: Earth Island Press, 1993).*

21

A Better Way to Measure the Economy

Ted Halstead

Since its introduction during World War II as a measure of military production, Gross National Product (GNP) has become the foremost indicator of national progress, and its increase has become the foremost priority of national governments. Continuing on this path, however, defies common sense and biophysical reality. Under current methods of economic accounting, maximizing GNP also results in maximizing social and environmental degradation. It is scientifically evident that the human economy, which is a subsystem of the biosphere, has already exceeded numerous biophysical limits to growth. But the central question is not between growth or no growth. We must differentiate the types and purposes of growth—growth of what, for whose benefit, at whose expense, based on what type and rate of resource use.

Since economic growth as measured by GNP does not account for depletion of the natural and social capital on which the future of the economy depends, our perception of increased economic health is a partial delusion. Yet it is this delusion that guides our economic course towards further environmental and social degradation. By valuing the goods and services that ecosystems provide to people and the economy at 'zero', the price system transfers the cost of environmental and social degradation from those responsible to society at large. When this nature-blind and person-blind accounting is combined with capital mobility, the profit motive induces capital to search out the most vulnerable communities and environments.

The Genuine Progress Indicator

At Redefining Progress we have developed a new system of measurement, the Genuine Progress Indicator (GPI), which is a measure of the general well-being and sustainability of the nation. In contrast to the GNP, which is merely a measure of economic production, the GPI takes into account both environmental and social factors. It is intended to give citizens a general guide to how well off we are as a nation, and how our national condition is changing over time. Because the GNP and the GPI are both measured in monetary terms, they can be compared using the same scale. Personal consumption constitutes the single largest element of both the GNP and the GPI. In contrast to the GNP, the GPI adjusts for the following:

1) *Resource Depletion*—A sustainable economy is one that supplies a physical base for economic activity for later generations. The GPI measures the loss of future availability of resources such as wetlands, farmland, and minerals as a current cost when these resources are depleted or degraded.

2) *Income Distribution*—According to economic theory, the value of additional income to the poor exceeds the value of extra income to the rich. The GPI rises when the poor receive a larger percentage of national income, and falls when their share decreases.

3) *Housework & Non-Market Transactions*—Much of what people value are the services we do for ourselves: e.g., childcare, cooking, cleaning and home repairs. These are ignored in official figures such as the GNP.

4) *Changes In Leisure Time*—As a nation grows richer, people should be able to choose between more output and more leisure. The GPI treats an increase in leisure as a benefit and decrease in leisure as a cost.

5) *Unemployment and Underemployment*—Many Americans are

unable to find a job or work as many hours as they need. The GPI counts the hours of chronic unemployment or underemployment as a cost.

6) *Pollution*—The GPI subtracts the costs of pollution as measured by damage to human health and the environment.

7) *Long-Term Environmental Damage*—Greenhouse warming and management of nuclear wastes are two long-range costs of nonrenewable energy use that do not show up in ordinary economic accounts. The GPI treats these deleterious choices as costs.

8) *Life Span of Consumer Durables & Infrastructure*—It is important to value the service received from durable items rather than the money spent on them. When you buy an appliance, for example, GNP records the value in the year of purchase, yet ignores how long it lasts. The GPI treats money spent to buy capital items as a cost and the value of the service derived from capital items as a benefit. This applies to both private capital items and to public infrastructure.

9) *Defensive Expenditures*—Funds spent to maintain a given level of service, without increasing the amount of service received, are treated as "defensive expenditures" (i.e., costs) in the GPI. Money spent on the medical and material costs of automobile accidents, and the money households spend on personal pollution control devices such as water filters are examples of defensive expenditures.

10) *Sustainable Investments*—If a nation allows its capital stock to decline or if it finances its investments out of borrowed capital, it is living beyond its means. The GPI measures net additions to the capital stock as a positive contribution to sustainable well-being and treats money borrowed from other countries as reductions in national self-sufficiency and sustainability.

For more information on the Genuine Progress Indicator, contact Redefining Progress, 1 Kearny Street, 4th Floor, San Francisco, CA 94108 (415) 781-1191.

Create Global Alliances

"If Americans wish to repair their own decayed democracy, they must also make themselves into large-minded citizens of the world. To protect their own economic interests, they will have to develop an interest in the economic conditions of people elsewhere.

... American democracy is now imprisoned by new circumstances—the dynamics of the global economy—and this has produced a daunting paradox: Restoring the domestic political order will require a new version of internationalism.

As a political system, the global economy is running downhill—a system that searches the world for the lowest common denominator in terms of national standards for wages, taxes and corporate obligations to health, the environment and stable communities. Left unchallenged, the global system will continue to undermine America's widely shared prosperity, but it also subverts the nation's ability to set its own political standards, the laws that uphold the shared values of society.

This reality constitutes the largest challenge confronting American democracy, one that underlies every other aspect of the democratic problem. The global economy has the practical power to check almost every effort Americans may undertake to reform their own political system—unless people learn how to confront the global system too. Elite political opinion holds that such resistance is undesirable and, in any case, impossible.

For ordinary Americans, traditionally independent and insular, the challenge requires them to think anew their place in the world. The only plausible way that citizens can defend themselves and their nation against the forces of globalization is to link their own interests cooperatively with the interests of other peoples in other nations—that is, with the foreigners who are competitors for the jobs and production but who are also victimized by the system. Americans will have to create new democratic alliances across national borders with the less prosperous people caught in the same dilemma. Together, they have to impose new political standards on multinational enterprises and on their own governments."

From William Greider, Who Will Tell the People *(New York: Touchstone, 1992), pp. 377-378.*

Stakeholders vs. Stockholders

Steven Hill

Today it is easier than ever for investors, corporate raiders, and their mobile capital to shop internationally for the highest yielding investments. The loss of a few hundred jobs in Scranton, Pennsylvania, or Flint, Michigan, or Tijuana, Mexico, is just a blip of information on their computer screens, like the trajectory of the latest stock quotes. Free traders are pitting disposable worker against disposable worker, state against state, and country against country.

The corporate raid, which had its heyday during the 1980s, remains a bitter and tragic affair, resulting in job loss and destabilization of the community where the company resides, as the major players tussle for control. Once the raider prevails, it's a simple matter to fire the workers, sell off the firm in parts and shift the proceeds elsewhere. In this era of global free trade, all the world appears to be a stage for the few players who control the capital.

Yet there have been pockets of resistance in the last few years to wheeler-dealer investors, corporate raiders and greedy free traders. Particularly interesting have been those episodes that have re-drawn the ideological battle lines in new ways. The partial antidote to corporate arrogance and autocracy has been to incite, not worker against worker as free traders would like, but affected communities and workers against capitalist greed. Five years ago, Pennsylvanians fighting against corporate raiders in their state found a friend in their state government.

Pennsylvania Fires a Shot

Pennsylvania's industries had been particularly hard hit in the 1980s by corporate raiders and takeovers. The state was still smarting over a 1984 attempt by T. Boone Pickens to acquire the Pittsburgh-based Gulf Oil Corporation through a corporate raid. His maneuvers ultimately drove the company into the arms of the Chevron Corporation of San Francisco, and Pittsburgh lost 1,500 jobs.

So when Canada's notorious Belzberg family attempted a hostile takeover of Armstrong World Industries in Beaver County in 1989, some legislators decided to fight back. They proposed the most sweeping anti-corporate takeover law in the country, raising the hackles of the financial conjurers of Wall Street.

In December 1989, articles began appearing in *The New York Times* and *The Wall Street Journal*, alerting the financial world to the new anti-takeover bill and precipitating a massive lobbying blitz in Harrisburg, Pennsylvania's capital. For the next eight months, articles and editorials appeared regularly in the business press, including *The Wall Street Journal*, *Forbes*, *Business Week*, *The Philadelphia Business Journal* and *The New York Times*, in most cases condemning the legislation. *Forbes* called it "socialism Pennsylvania-style," *Business Week* labeled it "a dangerous game," and *The New York Times* opined that the anti-takeover statute was the "sorriest example of state intervention." The mighty wallet of the financial world, including the United Shareholders of America, T. Boone Pickens, Chairman Richard Breeden of the Securities and Exchange Commission, and institutional (mutual and pension fund) investors like the $90 billion California Public Employees Retirement System condemned the anti-takeover bill and threatened federal lawsuits as well as an investor boycott of Pennsylvania.

What did this law aim to do, that it struck such a nerve? And who was it designed to protect? There were four provisions to the proposed bill. The first two were aimed squarely at corporate raiders attempting hostile takeovers. Raiders like Pickens were notorious for putting a company "in play" by buying large amounts of that company's shares and then threatening a take-over, causing corporate management to buy back the raider's shares at premium prices. If that sounds like a form of corporate blackmail, that's because it is—it's known as "greenmail." To address this, the bill limited the voting rights of any shareholder—such as a raider who controls 20 percent or more of a company's stock—to a maximum of 20 percent voting power. Then there was a "disgorgement" provision designed to make it unprofit-able for raiders to put a company into play at all. This provision enabled targeted companies to confiscate all of a shareholder's profits from shares sold within 18 months of a takeover attempt. Critics of the disgorgement provision said it would deter bona-fide buyouts or struggles for control of a company over legiti-mate management issues. Investors called this provision "wel-fare" for corporate managers, saying it would "entrench inept management at lazy local companies" (*Forbes*), invite "economic inefficiencies that could undermine competitiveness," (*Business Week*) and other investor nightmares.

Adding insult to injury from an investor's standpoint, a third provision of the Pennsylvania bill guaranteed 26 weeks' sever-ance pay for dislocated workers and the continuance of existing labor contracts once a hostile takeover bid had begun. This part of the bill attracted significant support from organized labor. "We feel corporate raiders are cannibals who financially attack healthy companies," said Bill George, a steelworker and then-secretary-treasurer (now president) of the state AFL-CIO. "Once a com-pany is in play, that starts the death dance on the corporation."

But perhaps the law's most interesting provision from a pro-gressive standpoint was the fourth, which allowed corporate managers who are facing takeover bids to consider not only the stockholders' interests, but also those of employees, customers, suppliers and the company's surrounding community—the "stakeholders." *Business Week* said this provision "undermined a key concept of capitalism: a board's fiduciary duty to share-holders." Translated, this means that the law took some influ-ence away from the absentee stockholders who often live hundreds if not thousands of miles from the community, and gave that influence to those who live in the community in which the corporation is based. Viewed in the context of global free trade, this provision represented a step toward "communitizing" multinational corporations, rather than nationalizing them.

Steven Wallman, the securities lawyer who drafted the legislation, said that this provision struck a middle ground between the interests of stockholders and stakeholders. "That provision was important, because it meant that corporate managers were no longer legally liable if they failed to 100-percent maximize the current share price. The manager's obligation is to act in the best interest of the corporation, but the stakeholder provision expanded the definition of what that means," says Wallman, now a commissioner for the federal Securities and Exchange Commission.

Socialism PA

More than any of the legislation's other aspects, the stakeholder concept caused the epithet "socialism" to be hurled disdainfully at the Pennsylvania state legislature. But red-baiting aside, the bill had overwhelming popular support, explained less by political or economic ideology than by populist local politics.

An unlikely alliance of politicians, business executives, organized labor and grassroots groups championed the bill as a means of protecting local jobs and communities. Weighing in as supporters of the bill were corporations and pro-business groups such as Westinghouse Electric, Scott Paper, Armstrong World Trade, Aluminum Corporation of America (ALCOA), and the Pennsylvania Chamber of Business and Industry—as well as the most powerful labor organizations in the state, including the United Steel Workers and the state AFL-CIO.

"We don't want to lose any more corporations to raiders," said Clifford Jones, then-president of the Pennsylvania Chamber of Business and Industry, a trade group that pushed heavily for the measure. Added Philip Lippincott, who was at the time the chairman and chief executive officer of Scott Paper: "This measure will eliminate greenmail, which is in everybody's interest. It isn't intended to eliminate a strategic buyer."

Despite investor threats of federal lawsuits and massive disinvestment, the bill passed resoundingly in both the Republican-dominated state Senate and the Democratic House. Amidst near-hysterical Wall Street predictions of financial doom, Governor Robert Casey signed the bill into law in April 1990.

More Than Meets the Eye

Besides the stakeholder provision, and the unusual alliance that pushed it, the Pennsylvania bill was intriguing for one other reason: it pitted the directors, managers, and CEOs of corporations against institutional and pension investors and shareholders, exposing a crack in the capitalist edifice. At the same time, the bill provoked a split between rank-and-file union members on the one hand, and union retirees and their pension funds on the other, threatening intergenerational labor solidarity.

These paradoxical trends bear watching as the economic tensions of free trade increase, since they may be indicators of shifting alliances. Is it possible that, as investors and pension fund beneficiaries seek to maximize their pension investment in the global economy, labor may not be able to count on its own pensioned retirees for solidarity and support? And is it possible that workers and organized labor may occasionally find allies in corporate managers, who are tired of being greenmailed by corporate raiders and taking the heat for chopping jobs in their local communities?

To be sure, each part of the alliance that pushed this bill had its own motives. And in some ways, it served the interests of management particularly well. There was some truth to the charge by investors that this law substantially removed stockholder oversight of corporate managers' performance. From a progressive or anti-capitalist standpoint, on the other hand, this was by no means a perfect law, since the "rights" granted to stakeholders could not be exercised by the recipients themselves. Instead, "benevolent" corporate managers were supposed to act in the stakeholders' interests.

Still, the theme of local politics—of protecting communities, stakeholders and jobs—prevailed because it had widespread Perot-style populist appeal. Pennsylvanians were mad as hell at Reaganomics and the takeover boom of the 1980s, and they weren't going to take it anymore. The theme of protecting communities from the excesses of capitalist greed rightly belongs to a progressive and socialist tradition, the legacy of Eugene Debs, Robert La Follette and others. And in a sure sign of its promise, the Pennsylvania plan struck a raw nerve in the financial and investment community. Yet progressive organizations and media have largely ignored this seminal event playing out in Pennsylvania.

Flash Forward, Five Years

Threats of federal lawsuits, disinvestment and boycotts from the United Shareholders of America and institutional investors never materialized, and the controversy over the law eventually died down. Years later, did the law have its intended effects?

"No question there's been a positive effect," says Clifford Jones, formerly president of the state's Chamber of Business and Industry. "At the time, it prevented the hostile takeover of Armstrong World Industries, Scott Paper and a few banks," says Jones. "The law made takeovers too expensive, and so the takeovers stopped." Specifically, Jones cites the successful use of the stakeholder provision by Armstrong World Industries as a defense in a lawsuit filed against them by the greenmailing Belzbergs. "Stakeholder provisions work, and now they are even being written into some corporate charters and bylaws," says Jones.

Dave Wilderman, from the state AFL-CIO, echoes this assessment, but a bit more cautiously. He notes that, of the 117 companies in Pennsylvania with capitalization over $10 million, 80 of these took advantage of a provision allowing a company to opt out of all or part of the law's requirements. These companies did this, most observers agree, as a result of heavy pressure from investors, particularly the California Public Employees Retirement System with its $90 billion worth of assets. Yet Wilderman still feels it was a good start. "There should be a greater role for community stakeholders in decision-making," he says today.

Stakeholders

The stakeholder provision may prove to be the law's most lasting effect. It introduced a truly radical notion—that of stakeholders—into the fray of corporate-community relations. Though none are as sweeping as the Pennsylvania statute, anti-takeover statutes and voting restrictions on large shareholders have passed in 23 states. Louisiana, Ohio and Texas, as well as some municipalities, have begun to require disinvesting companies to financially compensate abandoned communities and municipalities. Called "exit fees," these reparations are intended to provide for the diversification of the local economy, retraining workers, and the needs of the unemployed. In February 1993, at the urging of local government officials, Michigan Judge Donald Shelton issued a court order blocking General Motors' plans to relocate its Ypsilanti assembly plant to Arlington, Texas, asserting the rights of the "common welfare," in this instance the protection of local jobs (the order was later reversed upon appeal). Such community-affirming measures can be strengthened and broadened.

"Communitizing" the Economy

Measures like anti-takeover laws, exit fees, and stakeholder rights sketch the outlines of a new strategy to challenge the community-destroying aspects of global free trade and corporate raiders. Why shouldn't elected community and employee representatives sit as equals alongside stockholder representatives on the company board of directors? This would be an improvement on the German co-determination model of worker participation, forming a three-way economic "separation of powers" between owners, employees, and community members, much like the balance of power delegated to the executive, legislative and judicial branches of the U.S. government. And since corporations are such dominant players in our communities, why shouldn't voters help elect the corporate CEOs, the "executive" branch of these crucial institutions?

Stakeholder issues could have wide voter appeal, attracting anti-NAFTA support from the Nader left to the Perot right. If state legislatures prove unresponsive to lobbying, voter initiatives could attempt to mobilize entire communities, gathering signatures and raising awareness of the effects of global free trade and corporate disinvestment. While the globalization of the economy can seem like an inexorable trend inflicting inevitable damage, such campaigns provide a positive way for ordinary people to respond. Communities and states can effectively "communitize" multinational corporations by solidifying the legal framework of their stakeholders.

The Fair Trade Federation

*T*he Fair Trade Federation links disadvantaged producer groups in Third World countries with markets in North America. FTF is a membership organization that includes retailers, wholesalers, producer groups and concerned individuals working to educate consumers about the inequities of global trade and develop ways in which we can build an alternative system based on fair trade. FTF promotes fair trade practices such as:

• paying fair wages (in a local context) and distributing revenue equitably among producer group members;
• involving workers in the decision-making process and leadership positions, and striving to provide opportunities for worker ownership;
• using environmentally sustainable practices;
• being open to public accountability.

Members receive a quarterly newsletter (*NetWorks*), reduced rates on FTF publications such as their *Membership Directory and Resource Guide*, and the knowledge that they are helping to promote fair trade.

For more information, contact FTF at Box 126, Barre, MA 01005, (508) 355-0284.

The New Protectionism

Colin Hines and Tim Lang

The process of globalization is reducing the power of governments to provide what their populations require all over the world. Transnational corporations and international capital have become *de facto* the new world government, and their increasing control over the global economy is underpinned by the free trade orthodoxy. Existing world bodies, under the United Nations umbrella, already suffer a democratic deficit and are unable or unwilling to act before this New World Order.

We believe it is time to re-think the future direction of the global economy. The key issue is to put governments at a local, national and regional level back in control of their economies, and to relocalize and rediversify them. The reorganization of the global market that will allow such movement towards relocalized economies is what we call the New Protectionism.

First, two points of clarification. The New Protectionism, as we have formulated it, is neither anti-trade nor autarkic. Its goal is maximum local trade, within diversified sustainable local economies, and minimum long-distance trade; local is used here to mean a part of a country, and 'regional' a geographic grouping of countries.[1]

The key goal should be to build up sustainable economies. This requires a shift away from subjugating work to global pressures and markets. The purpose should be to build up diversified local economies, in place of the warehouse or global assembly line units of today.

Import and export controls: These should be introduced on a national and regional bloc level, with the aim of allowing localities and countries to produce as much of their food, goods and services as they can themselves. Anything that can't be provided nationally should be obtained regionally, with long-distance trade the very last resort. Goals should be set for each sector.

Controls on Transnational Corporations: TNC activities need to be brought back under government control. Market access should be dependent on compliance with a 'site here to sell here' policy. TNCs need to be broken up and subjected to greater transparency and shareholder power. Company and accounting law needs to control transfer pricing and the siphoning off of company profits and individual earnings off-shore.

Keeping capital local: With barriers to trade being dismantled and international capital flows virtually unfettered, national Treasuries have less and less control over their economic destiny. Money flies around the globe, when there should be controls on banks and pensions, insurance and investment funds to ensure the investment of the majority of funds in the locality where they are generated and/or needed, i.e., an 'invest here to prosper here' policy.

Competition policy: The domination by big companies is a feature of economic life which requires urgent debate. Many should be broken up, thus guaranteeing the local competition needed to maintain the impetus for improved products, more efficient resource use and the provision of choice.

Trade and aid for self-reliance: The GATT (General Agreement on Tariffs and Trade) should be revised to become a General Agreement for Sustainable Trade. Aid, technological transfer and the residual international trade should be geared to the building up of sustainable local economies. The goal should be to foster maximum employment through sustainable, regional self-reliance. The principle should be 'site here to sell here'.

Resource taxes: These would help pay for the radical economic transition, would be environmentally advantageous and would be politically feasible. Competition from regions without such taxes could be held at bay by re-introduced tariffs and controls. For the environment in general, relocalization would mean that adverse effects would be experienced locally, thus increasing the impetus and potential for control and improved standards.

Re-empowering government: In the name of globalization, government is inexorably shifting away from localities to the international level (and to TNCs). This needs to be reversed. Global institutions need a shake-up and the focus should be redirected to the local. Governments at the local, state and regional levels need to be able to bargain about access to markets and to foster more local savings and banking systems.

Differences Between the Old and the New Protectionism

A number of arguments are given against a New Protectionism. We address these in turn.

Some countries, such as England, live by trade and would die without it: This argument fudges the greater question: what sort of trade? When England was the dominant world power, the wealthy in England did indeed benefit by trade. Today, trade pressures are losing jobs, driving the deregulation of wages and social and environmental degradation, reducing elected governments control over their economies, and thus undermining the value of democracy. British society is dying *with* globalization, not without it.

Lack of competition is inefficient: This argues that consumers lose if companies are protected. Who wants expensive and shoddy goods and services? The scourge of inefficiency is competition. However, by assuming that giant corporations compete for purchasers' favors, the point that they shed workers (and therefore consumers) is lost. Also, by emphasizing local markets and limiting company size, the New Protectionism maintains the positive aspects of competition, i.e., the impetus to be cost competitive, utilize better design, and make more efficient use of resources. Lack of competition from those countries where wages, conditions and environmental laws are more lax will allow standards to be increased.

Even if it were desirable, no one country can go it alone. The New Protectionism cannot be achieved through autarky or go-it-alone policies. One argument currently being voiced is that the New Protectionism will emerge in affluent areas of the world, such as the European Union or North America, on the grounds that they are big and powerful enough markets to be able to dictate conditions to international capital and TNCs. Other regions would follow suit very quickly. Another argument is that the case for self-reliance emerges strongest at the periphery of an economy, just as we already see arguments for, and experience of, community self-reliance movements emerging in the battered post-industrial cities, or in the marginalized Third World. In either case, the future shape of the rapidly emerging regional trading blocks (EU, NAFTA, ASEAN, Mercosur, etc.) will both make the transition easier and be foci for debate about the future.

A fortress economy in the North would be unfair to the poor of the Third World who depend on trade to escape poverty: A handful of Third World countries, mostly in Asia, account for the vast majority of trade with, and receive most of the foreign direct investment from, the industrial countries. They could substitute this trade over the transition period to the New Protectionism globally by increasing their inter-regional trade. For the rest of the developing countries, and indeed for most of Eastern Europe, the present system forces such countries to distort their economies to produce the cheapest exports, usually in competition with other poor countries. Competition is not just setting poor against rich workers, but poor against poor.[2] This drains resources from meeting the basic needs of the poor majority in these countries. The key challenge is not to encourage further spirals of ruthless competition, but for Aid and Trade rules to be drastically rewritten so that they facilitate the building up and diversification of local economies globally. Only then will the needs of the poor majority be met.

The New Protectionism will pander to and play into the hands of right wing nationalism: We fear just the opposite. At present the adverse effects of the present globalization process for the majority's sense of security is leading to the spread of what could be termed 'free market fascism'. Only the hope and security offered by the New Protectionism can help reverse the very conditions which are fostering the rise of this ugly nationalist Right.

Protectionism failed in the 1930s, and it failed in communist countries everywhere: In the 1930s, protectionism was nationalist and designed to protect the powerful. The goal was for each protected industry or country to increase its economic strength and then compete at the expense of others. The more countries did this the less trade there was between them. The closed economies attempted by communist regimes were different from the New Protectionism in that the latter's internal competition and the international flow of ideas and technology will ensure that the stagnation and environmental degradation so often found in these regimes will not be repeated. The New Protectionism sets different goals: the minimization of the need to trade so much with other countries, if the traded goods and services can be met domestically. Why encourage a downward spiral of less diversity of economic activity within each country, which pits worker against worker and living standards against living standards?

Why should a radical change occur?

The simple answer is that unless people have work, hope and the promise of a decent quality of life, society is destabilized.

The globalization orthodoxy is caught in a double bind, pushed, on the one hand, to restructure and shed labor and pulled, on the other hand, by the need to have consumers. Already there is a murmur of voices against the orthodoxy. Even from within the supposedly successful Asian Tigers, there are strong critiques of the damage: rampant injustice, social dislocation, immoral inequality, insecure work and unemployment.[3] The message of the globalization orthodoxy is loud and clear. It tells people: you might not be needed.

We are not saying the clock can be turned back. Such a position would be nonsense. Our case is that with barriers to trade tumbling down, to the advantage of the global giants—companies and trading countries—the structural basis of the new Culture of Insecurity is laid bare. Insecurity on a scale not seen since the 1930s must be dealt with effectively; if not, history could repeat itself. One only needs to remember Mussolini's chilling pragmatism: "Fascism was . . . not a doctrine worked out beforehand in detailed elaboration; it was born of the need for action."[4]

The New Abolitionism

"We have to understand that it's what corporations are designed to do that is the source of their harm. We're saying it is illegitimate for corporate fictions to divide and conquer us; to define our labor; control our wealth; demarcate the commons; write our laws; elect our officials; poison our food; indoctrinate our children; use job blackmail and control of information, the press and money to run our local, state and federal governments. We're not suggesting that folks work harder to resist each chemical one at a time; each clear cut one at a time; each mass layoff one at a time; each toxic dump one at a time; each corporate purchase of a law or of an election one at a time. We're advocating citizen authority over the subordinate entity that is the modern, giant corporation... We are not about bestowing new rewards and incentives upon corporate leaders in order for them to cause a little less harm."

The above quote is by Richard Grossman who directs the Program on Corporations, Law and Democracy, P.O. Box 806, Cambridge, MA 02140, which promotes the idea that we should focus on challenging corporate charters: the underpinning of the legal fiction that confers on corporations the rights of human beings.

Conclusion: Building an Alternative

Kevin Danaher

As Tom Athanasiou says in his excellent book, *Divided Planet*: "Our tragedy lies in the richness of the available alternatives, and in the fact that so few of them are ever seriously explored." [1]

The technical means exist for feeding, housing and educating all the people on earth. The main problem confronting us is how to mobilize enough political will to overthrow the current system of elite rule and build a sustainable and equitable world economy. The goods news is that there are hundreds of groups struggling to create more democratic control of the capitol *and* the capital. What needs to be done?

• *Demystify the system and teach ourselves how to organize alternatives*. We need critical education about how the global economy really works: who benefits and who loses. The International Forum on Globalization in San Francisco organizes educational conferences and distributes useful educational materials on globalization. Call them at (415) 771-3394.

One of the most basic human skills—how to organize—needs to be taught in a systematic way so average citizens can create their own solutions to community problems rather than waiting for some distant 'leader' to do the job. Some of the better groups for helping your community get organized are included in the following list.

The Center for Third World Organizing trains community activists of color from across the country. Contact them at (510)

533-7583.

The Midwest Academy in Chicago runs 5-day seminars, "Organizing for Social Change." Contact them at (312) 645-6010.

ACORN (Association of Community Organizations for Reform Now) has a long track record developing community organizing skills. Their three main offices are in New Orleans (504) 943-0044, New York (718) 693-6700 and Chicago (312) 939-7488.

The Industrial Areas Foundation (IAF) is one of the biggest organizer training networks in the U.S., with branch offices around the country. Their main office is in Chicago (312) 245-9211.

• *Reform international economic institutions*. The World Bank and the International Monetary Fund (IMF) were originally chartered as part of the United Nations and were supposed to be under the control of the General Assembly (the more representative branch of the UN). But the global bankers now have complete control of these powerful bodies and they function to transfer wealth from the poor of the world to large banks and corporations. The 50 Years Is Enough Network has a detailed plan for restructuring these institutions to promote sustainable and participatory development. Contact them at (202) IMF-BANK.

• *We must develop ways to control the behavior of corporations.* There is already an international movement to create and enforce codes of conduct for transnational corporations. Government and citizens' movements have been pushing on many fronts to codify rules on how corporations can treat their workers, customers and the environment. A good group working to make transnational corporations more accountable is the National Labor Committee in New York (212) 242-0700. In 1995 they succeeded in forcing The Gap to reform the horrible working conditions in factories in El Salvador that produce clothing for The Gap. The Interfaith Center on Corporate Responsibility represents numerous church groups and uses shareholder activism to pressure corporations for change. Their newsletter, *The Corporate Examiner*, has useful information. Contact them at (212) 870-2936. Corporations exist only because we the people allow them to exist via charters issued by our state governments. If we could mobilize enough people to pressure our state governments, we could revise corporate chartering laws to impose codes of conduct or—in cases of corporate wrongdoing—we could revoke the corporation's charter and put them out of business. Some states already have this legislation on the books but there is not enough public awareness to exercise this restraint on corporate power. For more information on this strategy, contact The Program on Corporations, Law & Democracy, (508) 487-3151.

• *A tactic that has proven useful in many different struggles is boycotting corporate products.* For a comprehensive list of current boycotts and articles on strategy and tactics, see Boycott Quarterly ($20/year), Center for Economic Democracy, P.O. Box 30727, Seattle, WA 98103-0727. Another good boycott newsletter (*Boycott Action News*) is published as an insert in the *Co-op America Quarterly*, 1612 K Street NW, #600, Washington, DC 20006.

• *Special attention needs to be given to the environmental depradations of global corporations.* But it is not enough to focus public attention on specific misdeeds of corporations; it is necessary to criticize these misdeeds as part of a systemic tendency of corporations to put their own profits above the well-being of our planet. Groups we have worked with who are able to link practical action with a larger understanding of the need for system-wide change include: Rainforest Action Network, (415) 398-4404 has many campaigns, including one to pressure Mitsubishi Corporation to stop clearcutting tropical rainforests; the Student Environmental Action Coalition organizes college students on many global issues (919) 967-4600. Greenpeace still ranks as one of the more creative and militant organizations working on environmental issues. You can get local Greenpeace contacts by calling their Washington office at (202) 462-1177.

• *A key battleground for the corporations is the minds of our young people.* Corporations have penetrated the public school system with commercial messages and an ideolgy that extols profit-making as a civic virtue. A key group leading the resistance to this mind pollution is The Center for Commercial-Free Public Education, 360 Grand Ave., Suite 385, Oakland, CA 94610, (510) 268-1100.

• *We need a major restructuring of the U.S. tax system.* All taxes redistribute wealth: the question is, in which direction do we want that redistribution to go. To spur economic growth and more equity, we should demand a tax system that transfers wealth downward to the majority instead of upward to the minority. The former could lead us toward equal opportunity; the latter is leading us toward increasing class conflict and a deterioration of our society. Contact Citizens for Tax Justice, (202) 626-3780. For an accessible critique of the current U.S. tax system, see Donald L. Barlett and James B. Steele, *America: Who Really Pays the Taxes?* (New York: Simon and Schuster, 1994).

• Corporate power is nowhere more evident than in U.S. trade policy. Whether it's the struggle over NAFTA or efforts by big corporations to get Most Favored Nation (MFN) trading status for China, one of the best groups researching and organizing on these issues is Public Citizen. Its Global Trade Watch program can be reached at Public Citizen, 215 Pennsylvania Ave., SE, Washington, DC 20003, (202) 546-4996.

• *We must put the issue of inequality on the political agenda.* Most Americans are aware that inequality is getting worse but they lack specifics on just how bad the problem is and what we can do to fix it. For information on this central issue and what we can do about it, contact Share the Wealth (617) 423-2148 and ask for a sample copy of their quarterly newsletter, *Too Much.*

• *A growing number of groups are printing their own forms of currency as a way to strengthen local economies against the power of large corporations.* This strategy has worked quite well in Ithaca, New York and other places. To get an Ithaca Hours starter kit for $25, contact Ithaca Money, Box 6578, Ithaca, NY 14851. Other groups with information on local currencies include: LETS, c/o Landsman Community Services, Ltd., 1660 Embelton Crescent, Courtenay, BC, V9N 6N8, Canada (604) 338-0213; E. F. Schumacher Society, Box 76A, RD 3, Great Barrington, MA 01230 (413) 528-1737; or see *New Money for Healthy Communities*, by Thomas H. Greco, Jr., P.O. Box 42663, Tucson, AZ 85733.

• *Grassroots development organizations are building alternative economic institutions to provide jobs and include workers in decision-making.* The fair trade movement helps third world producer groups market their products in rich-country markets so they can work their way out of poverty rather than being dependent on charity. The Fair Trade Federation links fair trade organizations across North America to coordinate strategy and provide third world producer groups with more support. Contact them at (508) 355-0284. Transfair International is developing fair trade labels and links up progressive producer groups around the world. Call them at (612) 379-3892.

• *Get involved with the programs organized by Global Exchange to build grassroots internationalism.* Global Exchange sponsors a wide range of programs you can get involved with, including: Reality Tours to dozens of countries, a Fair Trade Program with three stores selling third world crafts, country specific campaigns to change U.S. policy toward Cuba, Mexico, Haiti and other countries, and we provide a broad range of educational materials and speakers. Please see the back pages of this book for more details. We can be reached at (415) 255-7296.

"*A human being is part of the whole called by us 'Universe,' a part limited in time and space. He experiences himself, his thoughts and feelings as something separated from the rest, a kind of optical delusion of consciousness. This delusion is a kind of prison for us, restricting us to our personal desires and to affection for a few persons nearest to us. Our task must be to free ourselves from this prison by widening our circle of compassion to embrace all living creatures and the whole of nature in its beauty.*"

Albert Einstein

"*Our loyalties must transcend our race, our tribe, our class and our nation; and this means we must develop a world perspective.*"

Rev. Martin Luther King, Jr.

"*And does activism even make a difference at the end of the day? Is there a happy ending? Well, hey, I'm one of the more pessimistic cats on the planet. I make Van Gogh look like a rodeo clown. And, with reluctance, I will say this—when you get involved, most probably, it'll suck at first. It'll be hard work with unclear results. But you know something? So what? That is life in all its glory. Life is not a movie. The right thing to do is simply get in the game. The price of apathy is too high to pay ... remember "We Are the World"? You want to see Dan Aykroyd singin' again? If only to prevent something like that from ever, ever recurring, please—get up off your ass, put some goddamn pants on and some undies, and* do *something.*"

Dennis Miller

Notes

Introduction: Corporate Power and the Quality of Life

1. *Corporate Power and the American Dream* (New York: The Labor Insititute, 1995) p. 6.

2. *Business Week,* May 14, 1990, p. 98.

3. See David Dembo and Ward Morehouse, *The Underbelly of the U.S. Economy: Joblessness and the Pauperization of Work in America* (New York: The Apex Press, 1995).

4. Quoted in "Multinationals and the Subversion of Sovereignty" *New Internationalist*, August 1993.

5. Anthony Lewis, "Budget Myths, Economic Realities," *San Francisco Chronicle*, January 13, 1996.

6. Donald L. Barlett and James B. Steele, *America: Who Really Pays the Taxes* (New York: Simon and Schuster, 1994), p.109.

7. Barlett and Steele, p. 51.

8. Barlett and Steele, p. 24.

9. Barlett and Steele, p. 97.

10. Barlett and Steele, p. 195.

11. See *Aid to Dependent Corporations*, (Washington, DC: Center for the Study of Responsive Law, 1995); and Chuck Collins, "Aid to Dependent Corporations," *Dollars and Sense*, May/June 1995.

12. For excellent reports on the inequities of the tax system and how it can be reformed, contact Citizens for Tax Justice, 1311 L Street, NW, Washington, DC 20005, (202) 626-3780.

13. See "Hostile Takeover: How the Aerospace Industries Association Gained Control of American Foreign Policy and Doubled Arms Transfers to Dictators" (Washington, DC: Project on Demilitarization and Democracy, 1995).

14. For extensive information on agribusiness, contact the Institute for Agriculture and Trade Policy (612) 379-5980.

15. Mike McNamee, "The GOP Had Better Get Business Off the Dole, Too" *Business Week*, October 16, 1995, p. 41.

16. *Business Week*, November 21, 1994.

17. Ronnie Dugger, "Real Populists Please Stand Up," *The Nation*, August 14-21, 1995.

18. *Newsweek*, February 26, 1996, p. 45.

19. "How High Can CEO Pay Go?," *Business Week*, April 22, 1996, p.101.

20. Edward N. Wolff, *Top Heavy: A Study of the Increasing Inequality of Wealth*

in America (New York: Twentieth Century Fund, 1995).

Chapter 9: Behind the Cloak of Benevolence: IMF/World Bank Policies Hurt Workers at Home & Abroad

1. U.S. Treasury Department, *The Multilateral Development Banks: Increasing U.S. Exports and Creating U.S. Jobs*, Washington, D.C.: May, 1994.
2. See, for example, the testimony of (then) Treasury Secretary Lloyd Bentsen before the House Appropriations Subcommittee on Foreign Operations, March 10, 1994 (Bentsen attributed 92,300 jobs a year to multilateral development bank policy-based lending); and the testimony of Treasury Under Secretary for International Affairs Lawrence Summers before the Senate Foreign Relations Subcommittee on International Economic Policy, Trade, Oceans and Environment, March 3, 1994.
3. National Labor Committee in Support of Worker and Human Rights in Central America, "Paying to Lose Our Jobs," September 1992, p. 7.
4. Adjustment and Equity in Developing Countries: A New Approach, a 1992 study by the Organization of Economic Cooperation and Development, quoted in "Assessing adjustment's social impact," *Africa Recovery*, August 1992, pp. 22-23.
5. *Ibid*.
6. Francois Misser, "Trade Unions and SAPs: Spending cuts could be better made elsewhere," *African Business*, June 1993, pp. 11-12.
7. Committee for Academic Freedom in Africa, "The World Bank and Education in Africa," *Race and Class*, Vol. 34, No. 1,1992, p. 57; the author cites data from World Bank, *World Development Report, 1990.*
8. International Labor Rights Education and Research Fund, *Worker Rights News*, Summer 1994, p.2.
9. Adapted from the Mozambique National Commission on Wages and Prices by Judith Marshall in *War, Debt and Structural Adjustment in Mozambique: the Social Impact* (Ottawa, Canada: The North-South Institute, 1992), p. 19.
10. *Ibid*.

Chapter 13: Global Ecology and the Common Good

1. James Gustave Speth, "Can the World Be Saved?," in Anthony B. Wolbarst, *Environment in Peril* (Washington: Smithsonian Institution Press, 1991), pp. 64-65.
2. Aldo Leopold, *The Sand County Almanac* (New York: Oxford University Press, 1949), p. viii.
3. The concept of the "treadmill of production" is taken from Allan Schnaiberg, *The Environment: From Surplus to Scarcity* (New York: Oxford University Press, 1980), pp. 205-50, and Schnaiberg and Kenneth Allan Gould, *Environment and Society* (New York: St. Martin's Press, 1949), p. viii. In Schnaiberg's earlier work the treadmill is situated in the historical context of monopoly capitalism as described in Paul Baran and Paul Sweezy's

Monopoly Capital (New York: Monthly Review Press, 1966) and James O'Connor's, *The Fiscal Crisis of the State* (New York: St. Martin's Press, 1973). It should be noted that the third element of the treadmill listed in the text above—the revolutionization of the means of production on pain of extinction—is attenuated in certain ways under monopoly capitalism, but still remains a general tendency of the system.

4. Schopenhauer quoted in Albert Einstein, *Ideas and Opinion* (New York: Dell, 1964), p. 20.

5. Chandler Morse, "Environment, Economics and Socialism," *Monthly Review* 30, no. 11 (April 1979), 12-15; Petra Kelly, *Thinking Green!* (Berkeley: Parallax Press, 1994), pp. 22-23. The tendency of the system to draw upon ever larger outputs of raw materials and energy was countered somewhat by increasing energy efficiency (measured by the ratio of GDP to commercial fuels consumed) in the advanced capitalist countries in the 1970s and early 1980s. Since the mid-1980s, however, progress in this respect has slowed as a result of falling energy prices. In the United States, which uses about as much energy as the entire Third World, energy efficiency has remained essentially unchanged since 1986. See Lester Brown et al., *Vital Signs 1992* (New York: W.W. Norton, 1992), pp. 54 -55, and *Vital Signs 1994*, pp. 126-27.

6. Speth, "Can the World Be Saved ?," p. 65.

7. C. Wright Mills, *The Power Elite* (New York: Oxford University Press, 1956), pp. 338-361.

8. Kevin J. Clancy and Robert S. Shulman, *Across the Board*, October 1993, p. 38; *The Statistical Abstract of the United States*, 1993 (Lanham, MD: Bernan Press, 1993), p. 147; "The Money Society," *Fortune*, July 6, 1987, 26-31; Bahro, *Socialism and Survival* (London: Heretic Books, 1982), p. 31; Rachel Carson, "Silent Spring—III," *The New Yorker*, 38, no. 19 (June 30, 1962): p. 67.

9. Alan Durning, *How Much Is Enough?* (New York: W.W. Norton, 1992), pp. 136-137; Jerry Mander, *In the Absence of the Sacred* (San Francisco: Sierra Club Books, 1991), pp. 78-79.

10. Paul Hawken, *The Ecology of Commerce* (New York: Harper Collins, 1993), pp. 1-2, 55-56, 216.

11. Noam Chomsky interview, Bill Moyers, ed., *A World of Ideas* (New York: Doubleday, 1989), p. 42.

12. Kenneth Galbraith, *The Culture of Contentment* (New York: Houghton Mifflin, 1992).

13. Petra Kelly, *Thinking Green!*, p. 25; Ben Jackson, *Poverty and the Planet* (Harmondsworth, England: Penguin, 1990), pp. 182-83; Raymond Williams, *Resources of Hope* (London: Verso, 1989), p. 221.

14. Quotation from Cheryl Payer, *Lent and Lost* (London: ZedBooks, 1991), p.115; also Susan George, "The Debt Boomerang," in Kevin Danaher, ed. *Fifty Years Is Enough* (Boston: South End Press, 1994), p. 29.

15. Foster, "The Limits of Environmentalism Without Class" *Capitalism,*

Nature, Socialism, 4, no. 1 (March 1993) 41; Thomas Dunk, "Talking About Trees: Environment and Society in Forest Workers' Culture." *The Canadian Review of Sociology and Anthropology*, 31, no. 1 (February 1994): pp. 14-34.

Chapter 22: The New Protectionism
1. Lang, T. and Hines, C., *The New Protectionism: Protecting the Future Against Free Trade* (London: Earthscan, 1993), p. 34.
2. See discussion of the trainer shoe market in *ibid.*, p. 80.
3. Bello, W. and Rosenfeld, S., *Dragons in Distress: Asia's Miracle Economies in Crisis*, (San Francisco: Food First, 1992).
4. Quoted in Palmer, R. and Carlton, J., *History of thc Modern World Since 1815* (New York: Knopf, 1971).

Conclusion: Building an Alternative
1. Tom Athanasiou, *Divided Planet: The Ecology of Rich and Poor* (New York: Little, Brown and Company, 1996), p. 307.

Index

Contributing Authors

Sarah Anderson is an Associate Fellow with the Institute for Policy Studies in Washington, DC.

Richard Barnet is a Senior Fellow at the Institute for Policy Studies in Washington, DC. He is co-author, with John Cavanagh, of *Global Dreams: Imperial Corporations and the New World Order*.

Robin Broad is a professor of environmental and development studies at American University and co-author with John Cavanagh of *Plundering Paradise: The Struggle for the Environment in the Philippines*.

Jean Anne Casey is a farmer in Oklahoma.

John Cavanagh is co-director of the Institute for Policy Studies, and co-author, with Richard J. Barnet, of *Global Dreams: Imperial Corporations and the New World Order*.

Noam Chomsky teaches at the Massachusetts Institute of Technology (MIT) and is a highly acclaimed author of dozens of books.

Peter Cooper works with Public Citizen's Global Trade Watch program.

Kevin Danaher is a Co-founder of Global Exchange in San Francisco. He is director of Global Exchange's Public Education Department.

John Bellamy Foster teaches sociology at the University of Oregon and is a member of the board of Monthly Review Foundation. His book *The Vulnerable Planet* was recently published by Monthly Review Press in New York.

Ted Halstead is the director of Redefining Progress, a research and public relations organization in San Francisco.

Steven Hill is a journalist and program coordinator of LaborNet at the Institute for Global Communications in San Francisco.

Colin Hines is co-author, with Tim Lang, of *The New Protectionism: Protecting the Future Against Free Trade*.

Colleen Hobbs is a writer.

Patricia Horn is an editor of *Dollars and Sense* magazine.

David Korten is Director of the People Centered Development Forum in New York and the author of *When Corporations Rule the World*.

Tim Lang is co-author, with Colin Hines, of *The New Protectionism: Protecting the Future Against Free Trade*.

Gayle Liles is a freelance journalist based in Fairfax, Virginia.

Jerry Mander is a senior fellow at the Public Media Center, and a co-founder of the International Forum on Globalization, both in San Francisco. He is the author of several books, including *The Case Against the Global Economy and For a Turn Toward the Local* (with Edward Goldsmith) from Sierra Club Books.

Russell Mokhiber is the editor of *Corporate Crime Reporter*, a legal affairs weekly based in Washington, DC.

Ralph Nader is a consumer advocate, author and founder of organizations such as Public Citizen and *Multinational Monitor*.

Jill Pike is an economist at the Institute for Policy Studies.

Jeremy Rifkin is the author of many books, including *The End of Work: The Decline of the Global Labor Force and the Dawn of the Post-Market Era*. He is president of the Foundation on Economic Trends, in Washington, DC.

James Rinehart teaches sociology at the University of Western Ontario in London, Canada and a member of the CAW (Canadian Auto Workers) Research Group on CAMI. He is the author of *The Tyranny of Work: Alienation and the Labor Process*.

Kirpatrick Sale is a contributing editor of *The Nation*. His most recent book, *Rebels Against the Future*, is an historical analysis of the Luddite movement and its relevance for today's world.

Norman Solomon is a syndicated columnist and author of several books critical of the corporate media, including *Through the Media Looking Glass: Decoding Bias and Blather in the News* (with Jeff Cohen).

Baldemar Velasquez is president of the Farm Labor Organizing Committee, AFL-CIO.

Lori Wallach is the Director of the Global Trade Watch program at Public Citizen in Washington, DC.

Andrew Wheat works with Ralph Nader's GATT Project in Washington, DC.

GLOBAL EXCHANGE

Global Exchange has what you need to get involved. Here are some of our programs.

• **Reality Tours**: We provide participants with a *feel* for the people of a country. We meet with farmers, human rights and peace activists, church workers, environmentalists, government officials and opposition leaders. We visit Cuba, Mexico, Haiti, South Africa, Ireland, Brazil, Senegal, Vietnam and other fascinating locations. We now feature domestic Reality Tours as well!

• **Public Education**: Global Exchange publishes books and pamphlets on world hunger, free trade vs. fair trade, the IMF & World Bank, Mexico, Cuba, Brazil and many other issues. We also make regular radio appearances, organize conferences and workshops, and sponsor public speakers. Our Speakers Bureau provides colleges and community groups with inspiring speakers on subjects such as Globalization, the World Bank, How to Work in the Third World, the World Food System and U.S. Farming, and U.S. many foreign policy issues.

• **Fair Trade**: To help build economic justice from the ground up, Global Exchange promotes alternative trade that benefits low-income producers and artisan co-ops. Sales at our Mill Valley, Berkeley and San Francisco fair trade stores support thousands of craftspeople in 30 developing countries and help educate people here in the U.S. about foreign cultures and international trade.

• **Material Assistance**: Global Exchange provides money and technical support to successful grassroots groups in Mexico, Cuba, Vietnam, Cambodia, South Africa, the United States and other countries. Our assistance has ranged from supporting a peasant-run literacy program in Honduras to providing scholarships for poor rural girls in Vietnam who would otherwise not be able to continue their education.

• **Human Rights Work**: By putting outside eyes and ears into conflict situations, Global Exchange helps expose human rights abuses and restrain repressive government forces. We arrange election observation teams, produce human rights reports and bring long-term volunteers into conflict zones such as the southern Mexican state of Chiapas.

Global Exchange works to create more justice and economic opportunity in the world. The heart of our work is the involvement of thousands of supporters around the country.

When you become a member of GX you get:
- our quarterly newsletter and Action Alerts;
- regular updates on our material aid campaigns and our support for development projects;
- priority on our Reality Tours to dozens of foreign countries and domestic destinations;
- a 10 percent discount on our educational materials and crafts sold at our third world craft stores;
- plus, you get connected to a growing global network of concerned citizens working to transform the world from the bottom up.

Please use the coupon below to join Global Exchange today.

- -

YES, I want to support Global Exchange's efforts to reform the global economy. Enclosed is my tax-deductible membership contribution.

____ $100 ____$50 ____$35 ____other

Name_____

Address_____

City_____ State____ Zip_____

Phone_____

GLOBAL EXCHANGE

2017 Mission Street, Suite 303, San Francisco, CA 94110
(415) 255-7296, FAX (415) 255-7498
email: globalexch@igc.apc.org